FROM
THERAPEUTIC JUSTICE
TO
FORENSIC COUNSELING

Dr. E. Scott Ryan, Ph.D.

Copyright@2006
E. Scott Ryan
All rights reserved

Edited by
Dawn Martin, RTO Board Member
Retired Teachers of Ontario
London, Ontario, Canada

ISBN# 0-9738786-0-6

Published in Canada by:
Forensic Counselling Associates, London, Ontario

Co-Sponsored by:
Forensic Enterprises, Lindsay, Ontario
and
Chosinness Productions, Toronto, Ontario

2nd Printing - 2007

E. Scott Ryan, or "Ted", earned his Ph.D. from the Rockefeller Graduate School of Criminology and Criminal Justice in Albany, New York. He was the first Woodrow Wilson Fellow in criminological conflict analysis, as well as the first Visiting Fellow at the United States Department of Justice in Washington, D.C. In addition to eight book publications in criminology, Dr. Ryan's studies as a criminal justician have been published in peer review journals of psychology, philosophy, education, forensics, theology, theosophy and political science inside and outside of the United States, to include Asia, Europe and Russia. He's served as the Charter and Emeritus Chair of the American Board of Forensic Counseling, and he has been appointed Co-chair of the American College of Forensic Examiners Task Force on Terrorism.

Dr. Ryan has also been a lifeguard, Army officer, and tenured Full Professor of Criminology. He recently earned his third degree Black Belt in the Korean martial art of Tae Kwon Do; and he was invited by the Head Coach of the United States Olympic Team to the Olympic Training Center in Colorado Springs to speak about the metaphysics of the world's largest Buddhist originated martial art. He credits his early Jesuit education as a young man with his later Masonic education as a not so young man. In his free time, he's an ardent advocate and demonstrator of survival swimming.

The author can be reached via email at eryan@mansfield.edu or on the Internet as Dr. E. Scott Ryan. His books are available at amazon.com under Dr. E. Scott Ryan.

CONTENTS

INTRODUCTION 1

CHAPTER ONE
Therapeutic Justice and Child Abuse 3

CHAPTER TWO
Forensic Counseling Rationality Classification 15

CHAPTER THREE
Cognitive Counseling in Criminal Justice 19

CHAPTER FOUR
The Criminal Belief Rationality: The Theology of Crime 25

CHAPTER FIVE
Futuristic Universal Metaphysics 47

CHAPTER SIX
*Case Studies of the Psychological and Forensic Assessment
of Parental Child Abuse* 63

CHAPTER SEVEN
Chosinness and the Theology of Terror 107

CHAPTER EIGHT
Forensic Counseling: A New Approach to School Crime 111

INTRODUCTION

The first chapter, Therapeutic Justice and Child Abuse, contains six case studies from the Commonwealth of Pennsylvania. One case was obtained from the criminal court files and is a matter of record. The other five cases were obtained from confidential court files and accessed at the request of law enforcement. All of these cases document how traditional therapeutic treatment has been employed in the justice system more as a substitute for justice than a supplement to justice.

The second chapter, The Forensic Counseling Rationality Classification, introduces a criminological based counseling system that allows for a more accurate assessment of criminal behavior. It indicates how criminal rationalities and associated criminal rationalizations can be determined without deterministic labeling.

The third chapter, Cognitive Counseling in Criminal Justice, presents a specific case analyst reporting guide to the classification and scoring of criminal rationalizations.

The fourth chapter, The Criminal Belief Rationality: The Theology of Crime, proffers a theology of crime multi-disciplinary analysis applying criminological, historical, psychological and theological references to the study of criminal belief rationalities. It first appeared as a professional monograph publication of The Journal of Instructional Psychology. Specific case studies, along with general policy analysis to include legal analysis, are presented with case study specific and general policy recommendations.

The fifth chapter, Futuristic Universal Metaphysics, was first published in philosophy, futuristic and education journals. Metaphysical criminological analysis is introduced with the new word, Chosinness, in describing the criminogenic metaphysics behind new and old ethnic and religious cleansings. Chosinness, as a new word, describes the sinful choice of choosing one God as one's God, only, to the detriment of others.

The sixth chapter, Case Studies on the Psychological and Forensic Assessment of Parental Child Abuse, was first published in a psychology journal after collaborating with a court appointed clinical psychologist in accessing his files. A forensic analytic critique of the process of applying psychological assessment to criminal cases is illustrated with five court cases from the State of New Jersey. The distinction between forensic and psychological analysis is presented along with recommendations for implementing new combinations of forensic and psychological assessment, analysis, diagnosis, classification and treatment.

The seventh chapter, Chosinness and The Theology of Terror, is based on the new word of Chosinness, defined as the sinful choice of choosing one God as one's God, only, to the detriment of others. It was first published in The Philalethes and The Education Journal. The metaphysical criminological construct of Chosinness is applied to the diagnosis of the metastasized belief systems that justify terrorism. The religious and political implications of Chosinness, in countering the criminal belief systems that produce terrorism on both the individual and state levels, are discussed.

The eighth chapter "Forensic Counseling: A New Approach to School Crime", was first published in <u>The Education Journal</u> and <u>The New Jersey Education Review</u>. Forensic Counseling seminars and workshops have since been conducted with various agencies and professional associations in Canada and the United States. As Charter Chair of the American Board of Forensic Counseling of The American College of Forensic Examiners, Dr. E. Scott Ryan was first asked to define forensic counseling, which he did in writing the first two books on the subject: <u>A Forensic Counseling Approach</u> (2001) and <u>Juvenile Forensic Counseling</u> (2002).

Thereafter, Dr. Ryan, as the first author, definer, implementer and agency originator of this new criminological approach as contrasted to traditional rehabilitative therapies, has worked on developing forensic counseling internationally as President of The International Institute of Forensic Education. He has also been invited to develop his forensic counseling approach in Canada, wherein he works with agency administrators, educators, politicians and mental health professionals via the Canadian-based Forensic Enterprises.

Forensic Counseling, as defined by Dr. Ryan, can be understood as counseling of offenders, either juveniles or adults, in a manner that does not repeat past treatment and education failures. Dr. Ryan describes the medical model treatment mistake of relying upon mental health professionals to treat crime and delinquency as if they were illnesses which could be cured.

These traditional therapeutic rehabilitative approaches have failed for the simple reason that an offender in trouble is not necessarily a troubled offender. Rather than repeating new variations of old therapies which are inappropriate, forensic counseling, as advocated by Dr. Ryan, concentrates on the specific criminal rationality dynamics associated with criminal rationalities and rationalizations. Participants in his forensic counseling seminars and workshops learn to encounter and counter criminal rationalities in a direct manner without denigrating the offender. The program objective is that of reversing criminal thinking and behavior patterns before they become worse with continued forensic counseling and treatment approaches. Forensic Counseling is both an art, in terms of individual proclivity and personal skill, and a science, in terms of applying correct criminological assessment, diagnosis, classification, interaction, treatment, follow-up and program development.

CHAPTER ONE

Therapeutic Justice and Child Abuse

In the United States, children die as a result of child abuse on a statistical average of more than one a week. There are countless others who suffer lifelong trauma and, quite often, today's abused child becomes tomorrow's abusing adult. Our society increasingly devotes more time, energy and resources in arguing the inarguable pro-life versus pro-choice debate as to the pre-born. On the other hand protection for our post-born children remains in virtual limbo.

One child abuse case in Pennsylvania, resulting in the torture-murder of a four year-old girl, Lee Ann Burrows, by her parents, occurred after the child had been removed as a result of abuse, and then returned to the parents. The girl was subjected to three weeks of beating terminating in her death. The child care caseworker, who was assigned to monitor the child's welfare, did not see the girl when she visited the child's family (due to her believing the lies, told by the parents, that the child was visiting her grandmother). The parents eventually - but tragically, too late for Lee Ann, found themselves in the Criminal Court, and both the father and mother were convicted of first and third degree murder respectively. When the parents appeared in court to sign a "voluntary" relinquishment of their "rights" to the two remaining girls, the mother was crying at losing her daughters while her husband waved, and in an attempt to console her said "What the hell, when we get out we will have more".

The details of the torture inflicted on the child are so gruesome that I will spare you the details other than the summation of the official pathological diagnosis:

1. Blunt impacts to head.
2. Blunt impacts to trunk.
3. Five pattern injuries of back and extremities caused by human bite marks.

4. Multiple contusions and abrasions of head, trunk, and extremities.
5. Pattern injury to head, trunk, and upper extremities.
6. Pattern injury of sole of right foot.
7. Contusions and laceration of external genitalia.

The place of therapy in our child protective justice system, according to the entrenched social work wisdom, is to enhance individual welfare and well being. Unfortunately, that is not often the case for abused children, while it is often the case for the child abuse offender.

As an introduction to the role of the so-called helping professions, one must seriously challenge the assumption that these two creatures, Mr. and Mrs. Burrows, who inflicted on their child what no animal of any species would ever do, have any rights left whatsoever, including the right to procreate.

Not having forfeited their right to life, which forfeiture, in my opinion, was warranted, at a minimum, sterilization should have been a condition of their sentence. Instead, the following psychiatric evaluation was contained in Mrs. Burrow's record:

At this time, I would feel that Mrs. Burrows represents most likely a personality trait disturbance, rather than any neurosis or any other diagnosis.

This therapeutic input into the justice system and Mrs. Burrows continued with an evaluation from a psychologist as follows:

Factors, such as self-assurance, determination, sociability, cautiousness in considering matters before making decisions, faith and trust in other people and energetic actions can be considered normal.

Lastly, the result of these evaluations was reflected in the following recommendation:

This woman would need continued counseling directed at mature choice of future husbands, if the other children are to be returned to her.

Fortunately, some unofficial arm twisting prevented her from keeping custody of her two other daughters and, thereby, having more children to torture, but were these therapeutic recommendations to have been followed, one can only surmise the resulting miscarriage of justice not to mention child abuse.

Throughout my research into this case, I could not but notice a glaring bias in these therapeutic evaluations as to "rights" for this murderer (she was convicted of third degree murder since her acts in torturing the child while contributing to the death did not actually cause it, rather, her husband delivered the fatal blows). The result of such an emphasis is a direct denial of the right to protection and in this particular case, the right to life, of abused children.

Our criminal justice and child protective systems, clearly, and indubitably, are not protecting abused children; changes are needed in stricter sentencing guidelines and better agency and court liaison along with more training for child case workers, physicians, police investigators, district attorneys, and judges.

In addition to better training for criminal justice practitioners such as the above, however, the role of therapeutic specialists needs particular scrutiny and drastic reconsideration. A form of benign, bureaucratic prejudice exists vis-à-vis the therapeutic professions such that our system operationally assumes that if the intention is good, the result will be good. As with any prejudice, such assumptions can be perfidious in their results even if they are not nefarious in their genesis. What has been described as the "Medical Model" in criminological studies is simply a professionally discredited prejudice based on an assumption that criminal offenders of the child abuse ilk, among others, are mentally ill or sick such that a therapeutic specialist can diagnose the illness and, as in medicine, provide a treatment-cure for this disease.

The major problem with the assumption behind the medical model is that it works. In fact, it does not work, and, further, there are scores of highly reputable studies from a variety of social sciences that prove it does not work. Nevertheless, our society continues to utilize vast amounts of taxpayers' funds to support the "Medical Model" approach under the guise that the so-called "helping" professions of social work and therapeutic rehabilitative counselors with degrees in psychology can somehow "help" i.e. "treat" these offenders after they're reported to law enforcement, child protective agencies, or the courts.

At the request of law enforcement experts, I obtained access to the confidential files concerning child abuse cases in a County Court in the Commonwealth of Pennsylvania. The Burrows case obtained from the Criminal Court files is a matter of public record: most child abuse cases, such as the following, never get that far.

I agreed to protect the identities of individuals since the files were classified as confidential, but, nevertheless, I decided to utilize information, verbatim, from the child abuse cases reported to this court. The reader should note that these cases occurred in one county located outside of any major metropolitan area such that by no means do they represent the result of a worse case scenario research project. In fact, the County Court where I conducted my research is on the same street that was once pictured in an advertisement in The New York Times as an example of an idyllic, American small town.

The first case concerned a six year-old girl who was abused by her mother's boyfriend with both passive and active participation on the part of the mother. The girl, I will call her Susan, was referred to Family Services in the Court because a pediatrician had noticed a third degree burn on her right eye, along with a broken pinky finger and missing hair. The exact wording of the case report was as follows:

The victim child had a third degree burn on her right eyelid, a broken pinky finger on her left hand, facial bruising, a sternal bruise in a non-weight bearing area, linear bruises in the lower abdomen and large patches of hair missing.

The child was removed from her mother and an emergency custody hearing was held granting temporary custody of Susan to Family Services. Susan was placed with a foster family and during the next five months, Susan, in her new supportive home environment, was able to relate further what had happened to her. In addition to her mother's boyfriend putting the hot tea bag on her eye resulting in third degree burns, the following abuses were reported to the Court by the foster mother with Susan's testimony:

The boyfriend punched Susan in the stomach; jumped on her while she laid on the couch; made her swallow a quarter, which she threw up (while he held her upside down); pulled her hair out; poked fingers in her eyes; held a lighter up to her fingers; bent her finger until he broke it; put his fingers in her privates.

What happened to the boyfriend? Nothing. He left the mother and the jurisdiction and was not charged. The psychological examination of this person, if you can call him that, concluded, The examination is not strongly suggestive of an individual who is prone to abuse others. The strongest indicator of any problem with this individual in the psychological report was as follows:

In general, he tends to be anxious and nervous and is likely to have a history of minor difficulties with social limits.

The child was returned to the mother. As in all of these cases, a series of psychological tests had been administered to both mother and boyfriend to include:

Melendez Neuropsychological Questionnaire
Soft Signs Evaluation
Wechsler Adult Intelligence Scale14
Minnesota Multiphasic Personality Inventory
Protective Figure Drawing Test
Word Association Test
Rorschach Psychodiagnostic Technique
Halsted-Reitan Neuropsychological Battery
Wide Range Achievement Test, and
Clinical Interviews

And what is the result of all of these supposedly scientific diagnostic instruments? Whereas one might expect some risk indicators of abusive tendencies on the part of the mother and at least serious warning as to the danger posed to the child by her mother, the following diagnosis appeared:

I would state that the mother is an anxious and threatened individual who is in dire need of developing a more positive self-image and insight into the dynamics of her heterosexual relationships. That is to say, the mother needs to understand why she tends to gravitate towards certain types of mates who are likely to be destructive to her.

The solicitous concern for the mother's sexual relationships at the expense of Susan's well-being is nothing less than that which would constitute scandalous malpractice in any other profession. Obviously, protection can not be provided for child victims with this kind of inane diagnosis from the therapeutic so-called specialists.

The next case involved a 33-year-old father, whom I have named John, who sexually abused his 15- year-old daughter, Jennifer. The investigative report concluded as follows:

The perpetrator admitted to undressing the victim child and self, fondling victim-child's breasts and genitals, performing cunnilingus on victim-child, having victim-child fondle his penis to erection and ejaculation, and partially inserting his penis into victim-child's vagina.

You might wonder how many years John served in prison for his admitted sexual abuse of his own daughter. I wondered, too, until I discovered that he received no sentence whatsoever—instead he was placed in therapy!

The Licensed Clinical Neuropsychologist, handsomely reimbursed with our taxes, apparently assured the District Attorney with his diagnosis that "with appropriate treatment, I would consider his (John's) prognosis to be essentially favorable....John should enter psychotherapy to provide him with supportive counseling."

The psychological report centered around John's guilt about having had an affair with his wife's sister and his despondency over his wife's tit-for-tat extramarital affair in revenge for his all-in-the-family escapade. While some of this material might provide a titillating script for a soap opera, there was nothing that could be found as a risk indicator for protecting his daughter from a probable later recurrence.

In the following case, thirteen year-old Diane was sexually abused by her mother's paramour, fifty-nine year-old Jack. The record contained the following descriptive conclusions as to Jack's abuse of Diane:

1. Fondling and kissing child's breasts on more than one occasion.
2. Fondling child's genitalia, and inserting his finger on more than one occasion.
3. Performing cunnilingus on child.
4. Attempting to have intercourse on one occasion, but not succeeding.

This abuse occurred when Diane lived with her mother for a short time between September and October. Diane was removed during the evenings and placed in the overnight custody of her grandmother. On November 8 of the same year (approximately one month after being abused and being removed from her mother), she was returned to her mother and then removed once more after being abused again. The report of the M.S.W. (Masters in Social Work), I have named him Mr. Baxter, that returned Diane to more of the sexual abuse that she had just recently been removed from had contained the following:

I'm pleased to report Diane, the mother, and Jack have made significant gains in treatment and I can recommend removing the restriction that Diane spend overnights with her grandmother.

If this criminally negligent charade of professional decision making were not enough, another consulting therapist later assigned to Diane, this time an M.A. in Psychotherapy, wrote:

At this point (six months after Diane had been removed a second time), I would recommend Mr. Baxter (the first therapist) foremost to handle the treatment for Diane and her family. So now, not only was the criminal negligence of the previous therapeutic diagnosis by Mr. Baxter ignored, it was, in effect, therapeutically sanctioned with the second therapist's recommendation of continuing the foremost role for the first therapist, Mr. Baxter, who had therapeutically sentenced Diane to a continuation of what was known and documented sexual abuse.

I began to understand the frustrations of law enforcement sources who had asked me to study this process as an independent and non-agency affiliated criminologist. This particular case, however, highlighted not only an egregious lack of child protection and a grossly negligent distortion of professionalism on the part of the social workers and psychotherapists; but, further, it reflected an arrogance that goes far beyond normal stupidity.

In my experiences with self-inflated professionalisms (whether they be couched in lawyers Latinized or therapeutic Freudianisms), I have found most of them to be illustrations of outward arrogance camouflaging a basic deficiency in the individual and/or the profession. As in the case at hand, the therapist assumed a posture of attempting to obfuscate the basic lack of relevant knowledge in the pseudo-profession of therapy and intellectual impotence in the individual therapist by further, arcane diagnosis.

Rather than the reader relying solely on my interpretation, a continuation from the court records of the therapeutic recommendations is proffered: Regarding the sexual abuse these two (mother and her boyfriend, Jack) have a very complicated situation which they have not been able to communicate openly about with one another... The mother has not resolved for herself what this means to her relationship with her boyfriend and with Diane, although she is strongly committed to Diane.

The mother and boyfriend had left the jurisdiction with Diane and were planning to return from their Florida vacation.

The therapeutic recommendation continued:

If Diane and her mother indeed return this summer, I strongly recommend both individual and family therapy for both Diane and her mother to work in the direction of the following goals:

1. Open communication and decision-making regarding Diane's sexual

abuse and its impact on all relationships involved (to include the boyfriend).
2. Increase Diane's responsibility for her behavior and control of her temper.

In a remarkable display of amazing callousness towards the victim, the therapist singled out Diane for responsibility training and temper control instruction. Yes, imagine if you will, this abused girl becoming very upset, as any normal person might, while the therapist counsels the mother on "communicating more openly" with her boyfriend. In this instance one can observe, from any moral or rational perspective, a most twisted irony and travesty of justice in the ludicrous therapeutic concern for the mother's relationship with the abusing boyfriend and critical admonition for the sexually victimized daughter.

The woman's movement has adamantly critiqued the "blame the victim" reaction in our legal system to all too many female rape victims. In this illustrative example of Therapeutic Justice, we see another form of abuse against a young girl wherein the victim is blamed for getting angry and losing her temper, while the therapist counsels and consoles the offender and his abuse-enabling girlfriend and mother of the victim.

The following case involved a five year-old boy, whom I have named Peter, who was sexually abused by his mother's bi-sexual boyfriend. The description of the injuries were as follows:

Male perpetrator put his "pricker" in child's rectum. Male and female perpetrators put other things in child's rectum. Perpetrators performed fellatio on the child.

Numerous complaints as to Samantha, the mother, and her boyfriend, George, abusing her son had been reported before they surfaced in the court as a case of child abuse resulting from a custody fight for the child.

The mother, who had herself been sexually abused as a child, at a minimum, tolerated the sexual abuse of her son and most likely participated in most of the abuse.

This time the therapeutic diagnosis was written by a Ph.D. in psychology. The diagnosis from this licensed psychologist as to any deficiencies in the mother was as follows:

Her weakest attributes appear to be in areas which concern interpersonal relationships and expression of feelings thereof. She appears to be one who strongly desires to have positive relationships with her children and members of the opposite sex, but may very well not be able to provide all that is needed in fulfilling relationships, as her needs as of yet have not been met. She is strongly desirous of a lot of love and attention and affection.

The rest of the therapeutic diagnosis contained the following:
She does seem to have a feeling of family unity and does have ideas about

how to positively interact with her children...As a matter of fact, she is an intelligent individual who appears to have the capabilities of appropriately parenting and providing for her children.

Based upon this evaluation, the following recommendations were made:

There are no elements of the client's personality which would suggest that she presents as an immediate and ongoing threat to the well being of her children, particularly her young son, Peter. Even though elements of impulsivity, compulsivity and poor self-concept have been indicated in this evaluation, the client's behaviors have not substantiated the presence of these features on a consistent and ongoing basis such that they present harm or detriment to her children.

Luckily, as a result of the custody battle the abuse was further documented. If the Court had relied solely on the psychological evaluations, five year-old Peter would still be the victim of sexual abuse.

The next case of a little girl whom I have named Edith, aged four, was one wherein the child was removed from the custody of her retarded, natural parents at birth. She was placed with foster parents and then returned to her natural parents at eight months. She was thereafter removed again at almost three years due to recurrent abuse.

The natural parents shortly prior to her fourth birthday wanted her back. The foster parents were fighting to retain custody of Edith since the caseworker, the seventh one to work on this case in four years due to high caseworker turnover, recommended return to the natural parents.

The abuse that the child underwent in the custody of her natural parents was recorded as follows:

Medical examination of the victim child revealed large introitus with the hymenal ring definitely stretched. Physician noted this was an abnormal genital examination. Child became very excited, screamed and held her legs together when doctor attempted to examine her. She reacted the same whenever anyone tried to change her diaper. The victim child's parents claim no knowledge of what happened to their child. They claim the child was rarely, if ever, out of their sight. Parents are listed as perpetrators.

Upon interrogation of the mother, she admitted to pushing a wash-cloth into the baby's privates stating "that's the way her parents did it to her."

With all of this evidence of previous abuse, I wondered why the case-worker recommended returning Edith to her natural parents. Accordingly, I was able to arrange for an interview with the caseworker. She turned out to be the typical child caseworker: young, overworked, underpaid, burnt out and looking for another job. Perhaps, since she was planning to leave in the next month, she could afford to be candid with me?

During my cross examination of the caseworker she admitted to me that the natural, retarded mother had no desire to change; she was compulsive in her behavior; and that it was quite possible that she would revert sooner if not later to her sexual abuse of Edith. Why then the recommendation?

Inexorably and incredibly, she was instructed to carry out the return of the daughter to her mother upon the mother's successful completion of a one year sexual therapy program. Since the mother had successfully completed the therapy (even though she was still a danger to the child), she was instructed to complete the therapeutic contract in returning the child to her mother.

Fortuitously, the right thing happened for the wrong reason, and for the first time in my research, I was grateful for influence peddling in our legal system. The foster parents were wealthy, influential members of the country club to which the presiding judge belonged and their wishes prevailed and Edith was spared yet another period of sexual abuse from the retarded parents.

Of course this unusually happy ending provides no consolation when, as can be the case, the abusing parents also belong to the country club.

I have shown some examples of what is occurring, and what should not be happening in any country, in just one, all-American, idyllic, small town in Pennsylvania. I'm not espousing prejudice against any and all treatment approaches: wherein treatment is defined as any valid and effective way of improving a situation and not proscribed and circumscribed, as is done now, to therapeutic social work and psychological treatment concepts based on the Medical Model. However, I have presented documentation sufficient to justify the need for post-justice - implying major changes based after (not before) the facts in the policy and practice of relying upon Therapeutic Justice in child abuse situations, in particular, and in the justice system, in general.

After researching these cases, I felt a sense of personal outrage and national shame knowing that this problem, endemic throughout the nation, comprises hundreds of thousands of four year-old Ediths, five year-old Peters, six year-old Susans, thirteen year-old Dianes and fifteen year old Jennifers.

One hope from and advantage of the publicity from the Joel Steinberg trial in New York City is public awareness that this problem is not limited to the inner cities nor absent from the middle class and small town, U.S.A. The next step is to recognize that our system of relying on therapeutic diagnosis and recommendations in child abuse cases helps neither the child nor promotes justice. In fact, what I've termed Therapeutic Justice is a pseudo-scientific farce that postures therapy for victimizing clients at the expense of protection for victimized children. If I may paraphrase The Talmud, showing toleration to the cruel is showing cruelty to the innocent. If we continue with our present system of Therapeutic Justice, our society has violated this Talmudic principle along with any other standard of decency.

In the case of six year-old Susan, this distortion of Therapeutic Justice not only ignored major diagnostic errors, but perpetuated them by emphasizing self-understanding for an offender resulting in continuing physical and sexual torture for a six year-old girl.

In the case of Jennifer, the emphasis of this therapeutic blight on our criminal justice system provided supportive counseling to treat the guilt complex of the abusing father and nothing for his victimized fifteen year-old daughter.

In the tragic and incredible case of Diane, Therapeutic Justice blamed the thirteen year-old victim for being angry, and provided therapy to help the abusing mother and boyfriend "understand" their relationship with each other.

In the case of five year-old Peter, the term "client" was constantly used for the abusive mother while the safety of the victim child was ignored.

Lastly, four year-old Edith was almost delivered back to her parental abusers for further unspeakable perversion solely because the offending party completed the treatment contract that Therapeutic Justice mandated.

Is the solution more money? My answer is "NO"!

Rather, I suggest that 50% of all United States Department of Justice and state criminal justice research funds be immediately diverted to opening the confidential files of family, juvenile and child service cases to operational (not academic) research and monitoring.

Academic research in the justice system, which examines interrelationships among variables according to stipulated social science methodologies, most often, produces results that are, at best, esoteric and usually irrelevant or meaningless. A strong dichotomy exists between this kind of traditional academic research, which despite governmental deficits still receives allocations in the millions, and operational research, which is NOT being adequately funded.

Simply and to the point, a rampant life-threatening problem through-out our society for child victims continues to remain unaddressed. There is a drastic need to utilize governmental research funds in a way that can affect and change the decision making and administrative operations of our justice system and child protective agencies. The government should change its policy of funding academic studies and focus on accessing information (rather than academic research data in the form of statistical variables) with which others can follow through with systemic intervention mechanisms at critical stages of decision making in agency operations.

Thereby, Therapeutic Justice along with other systems dysfunctions can be monitored and, where necessary, as in the case of Therapeutic Justice, completely removed from the system. Without a drastic change in research policy, governmental funded research only contributes to the status quo ante and produces recommendations that are deja vu and protective of the bureaucratic sacred cows. Forbid that a particular researcher be identified as NEGATIVE, i.e. threatening to the self interests of those who profit from the false and dysfunctional solution of Therapeutic Justice at the expense of effective problem solving.

On the state level, a child-protective Ombudsman (a private individual who is authorized to overview a public problem) should be appointed by every Governor to report on the progress of child protection in every jurisdiction of every state.

Most investigative and governmental inquires into problems of the justice system have tended to assume the "rotten apple" methodology wherein individuals are identified as wrongdoers and, thereafter, the problem is dismissed. The difficulty with this tried and less than true approach is that it provides immediate satisfaction and the illusion of solving a problem while the underlying systems basis of the situation is overlooked. The task in solving the problem of dealing with child abuse is not solely that of ferreting out a few rotten apples in the barrel, but rather, one of recognizing, metaphorically, that the barrel itself is rotten.

Our society's child victims are undergoing preventable abuse not because of rotten people who staff our agencies but because of a rotten system of Therapeutic Justice. Confidentiality for child victims is justified, for the justice system and its' bureaucracy, however, it is a contributor to child victimization, an accessory to child abuse.

In addition to operational research, a private Commission should be created by the Congress and the President to review on a yearly basis needed changes in our laws and administration of justice and child protective services. This task of this Commission should include elimination of the pseudo-professional golden calf and administrative sacred cow of Therapeutic Justice which is a major factor in contributing to injustice for all, but most of all, our abused and murdered children.

CHAPTER TWO

Forensic Counseling Rationality Classification

The author presents a counseling system which enables one to employ criminological treatment approaches with greater cognitive clarification. This system allows for reality based assessments of criminal behavior and associated criminal rationalities without any deterministic labeling. The purpose of this classification system is that of a realistic and collaborative identification of criminogenic thought and behavior such that more accurate cognitive treatment approaches can be generated with respect for change and responsibility in the offender.

The criminological assessment of the helping professions has been that of being less than helpful in terms of rehabilitating criminals (in returning them to society) or in habilitating criminals (in turning them towards a non-criminal society they have never been a part of). With the exception of those vocational counselors who do actually find gainful employment for their criminal clients, counseling has not worked to such an obvious extent that, today, many professionals as well as laymen in the criminal justice system assume that nothing works, and that nothing can work.

The knowledge, however, that therapy based on the medical model of corrections (a scientifically discredited prejudice based on the assumption that criminal offenders are mentally ill or sick such that a therapeutic specialist can diagnose the illness and, as in medicine, provide a treatment/cure for the disease) does not work, does not mean that we know that any and all treatment cannot work. It simply means that we know that "therapeutic justice" (therapy according to the medical model applied in the justice system) has been regarded as a sacred cow and golden calf for too long by too many, to the detriment of just treatment and our treatment of justice.

Just treatment, first and foremost, is any treatment that is just in first recognizing and objectively classifying the primary processes of criminal offenders.

Last and least, it does not rely on the subjective interpretations of therapeutic justice, as does much Freudian neopsychology in what I describe as fraudulent neo-Fraudian psychology. Further, the treatment of justice – in treating both the victim and victimizer with justice – can be successfully implemented with a collaborative educational approach, rather than with any singularized clinical approach.

Criminological studies have scientifically demonstrated that treatment based on analysis of the subconscious mind is not just unhelpful but unjust and false. It is unjust for both victim and victimizer and false in the overwhelming majority of criminal cases, in terms of effective counseling and correctional problem solving intervention. On the basis of extensive criminological data, a variety of counter therapies in criminologically countering the behaviorism of therapeutic encountering with behavioral accountability have arisen in countering traditional therapy. These criminological treatment approaches, some of which are quite new and some quite old are most often described in terms of accountability, confrontation, reality and responsibility. Therapies include shock corrections programs in assorted correctional "boot camps" and in other correctional alternatives to what can correctly be termed non-correctional/correctional institutionalization. What distinguishes these criminological treatment approaches is their primary and often exclusive emphasis on behavior as the single and total measure of analysis, classification and treatment.

It is not my purpose in this article to present all the strengths and weaknesses of these criminological treatment approaches - other than to present the basic fact that they have both an immense strength and an immense weakness. Their strength proceeds from the fact that they have freed themselves from the medical model pharmaceutical prescriptions of the oft-tried and just as often untrue non-curative treatments of therapeutic justice. Their weakness, however, is that they have tended to throw out the baby with the bathwater...in throwing out the conscious baby of the conscious mind with the unconscionable bath water of the unconscious mind.

In other words, in reacting to the Freudian abuses of therapeutic justice, they have left out necessary analysis, classification and treatment according to the real measure of the conscious criminal mind. The fact that criminal treatment did not work when it was based on the false measure of Freudian analysis in therapeutic justice has been extended from that of a true fact to a false assumption, such that any analysis, classification and treatment of the criminal mind, at present, tends to be regarded as verboten. Like any assumption - verboten or otherwise - this assumption rests more on one's fear of repeating past mistakes then in facing what's necessary, now, and in the future.

Accordingly, in exercising my own present and futuristic assumptions in this regard, I've presented a cognitive classification system that allows one to incorporate analysis of the criminal mind i.e. the conscious mind, in conjunction with non-therapeutic, criminological treatment programs. This total cognitive approach is total even in regard to the non-cognitive, in also classifying the non-cognitive for the purpose of criminal justice practitioners being better able to recognize and refer these minority of criminal cases to appropriate mental health practitioners.

Nevertheless, the cognitive criteria of objective behavioral measurements is never abandoned nor compromised with the subjective behavioralist criteria of therapeutic justice.

This total thinking classification which I originally entitled "The Cognitive Gestalt Classification" has been in use in a variety of treatment settings for both adult and juvenile offenders and for substance abusers as well as those classified with mental health problems. For the purpose of introducing this treatment approach for wider application, I decided to change the title to "Cognitive Counseling in Criminal Justice." The reason for this change in title is purely semantic, in that a number of counselors who had experienced their own problems with therapeutic justice expressed their aversion to the German word "Gestalt" in associating it with the psychological Austrian world of Sigmund Freud. Furthermore, many correctional counselors went even further than I did in my own Fraudian description, to disclose their own Fraudian experiences with therapeutic justice in terminology not quite suitable for disclosure in this article.

Accordingly, therefore, this system of cognitive analysis, classification and treatment is presented for implementation in conjunction with criminological programs based on behavioral accountability. The cognitive emphasis of this system is presented as a supplement, in fact a necessary supplement, to behavioral intervention rather than as a substitute - least of all a "therapeutic justice" substitute. In applying cognitive counseling, it's strongly recommended that any treatment unit or team consist of no less than three practitioners who are able to closely observe the offender's behavior and to interact with the offender in an intensive interpersonal manner.

The following is a case analyst guide to the cognitive classification and scoring of criminal rationalities along with suggested reporting mechanisms. As mentioned at the end of the guide, and what bears repeated mention throughout, in the utilization of this cognitive adjunct to any treatment plan, is that unlike some other treatment plans, the classifications herein are meant to be fluid rather than static. Their purpose is to assist the counselor in helping the criminal offender to map out how to change in changing his or her criminal rationalities. Therefore, at no time in the treatment process should any classification score be interpreted or presented as a deterministic, behavioralistic or final label. To conclude my introduction to this cognitive counseling plan: this classification is a map pointing to directions for change with the status of change being continually in flux depending on the interpersonal dynamics of the counselor, the treatment unit, and the offender.

The only guarantee of success, herein, is the guarantee that this classification system does not perpetuate the failure of "therapeutic justice."

CHAPTER THREE

Cognitive Counseling in Criminal Justice

CASE ANALYST GUIDE TO CLASSIFICATION AND SCORING OF CRIMINAL RATIONALITIES AND REPORTING

The first score, referred to as the Bump Score, indicates the degree of seriousness of the offender's difficulties, brushes or bumps with society that led up to his appearance within the juvenile or criminal justice system. In order to arrive at an accurate Bump Score, the analyst must be fully aware of the offender's social and personal history. The Bump Score should comprehensively and realistically reflect the percipient processes, both formal and informal, that were instrumental in and reflective of the criminogenic development of the offender.

Scoring for the Bump Score and further scoring should be based on the following standard:

1. Low - minor or less serious
2. Medium - getting serious
3. High - serious
4. Very High - extreme seriousness such that the offender appears to a gone or "never fit" case.

While one analyst may allocate a 2 to what another may evaluate as a 3, the controls for standardization are the full case accounts that the analyst must present to explain the basis for the scoring of the offender's tension with society.

Every score must be fully explained, documented and illustrated with behavioral information (the offender words and actions) rather than with questionnaire or psychological instruments.

After the Bump Score with case explanation and illustration, the analyst shall apply the same scoring to a series of rationalities or cognitive processes associated with the criminogenic behavior of the offender.

There are five rationalities in the model:

1. Functional Rationality
2. Belief Rationality
3. Ideation Rationality
4. Group Rationality
5. Inevitability Rationality

These rationalities are not mutually exclusive and an offender may have more than one rationality. As with the Bump Score (BS), the Rationality Score (RS) must be fully explained and illustrated based upon behavior. An introductory explanation of these rationalities follows:

1. <u>The Functional Rationality</u> - The offender's reasoning is one of the end of self interest justifying any means. Whatever is instrumental or functional in achieving the interests, desires, or wants of the offender is reasoned as good or appropriate regardless of the consequences to others.
2. <u>The Belief Rationality</u> - The offender's reasoning responses are either bracketed or determined by a belief premise. A person with this rationality does not reason why or question or evaluate - he or she blindly follows the revealed or mandated dictates. Many cult members fall in this category.
3. <u>The Ideation Rationality</u> - The offender's reasoning is based upon an ideology, thought system or philosophy. The goals or explanations of the thought system not only guide reasoning and behavior but are such that they produce a patterned response. However, this patterned response is not to be equated with the conditioned response of cult members. Terrorists are prime examples of criminal ideation rationality; whereas the cultist follows a creed or revelation or commandment, the terrorist explains the mental basis for his calculated and reasoned response by pointing to either a real or imagined injustice. The injustice or social good is usually described in such a way that only violence or crime are seen as remedies or justified responses to the desired end.
4. <u>The Group Rationality</u> - The offender reasons that what is good for the group is right or at least not wrong - no matter what is done. Certain motorcycle gangs, syndicate organized crime families and power elite criminals are conspicuous in this category. The adage that "what's good for G.M. is good for the country" when applied to justifying the deliberate manufacture of unsafe automobiles is a documented example of the power elite brand of this rationality.
5. <u>The Inevitability Rationality</u> - The offender reasons that he is "not in control." No matter what is done, things are bound to happen and prospects for change are practically nonexistent.

There are four sub-categories of this rationality:

(a) Mental Disease
(b) Mental or Emotional Disturbance
(c) Criminality of the Addictive
(d) Addictive Criminality

(a) <u>Mental Disease</u> - In accordance with scientific critiques of the mental illness model, mental disease is utilized rather than the pseudo-scientific, psychological classification of mental illness. Diseases of a brain or bio-chemical nature that affect reasoning such that an offender did not know reality or what he did are acknowledged as an inevitability rationality. However, such a diagnosis must be scientifically verified either in its genesis or manifestation.

(b) <u>Mental or Emotional Disturbance</u> - When a mental or emotional disturbance is severe enough to affect perception of reality such that those perceptions translate into criminal behavior, the offender has an inevitability rationality. The contention of determined behavior is not postulated unless as with mental disease, it can be scientifically verified. More often than not the disturbance functions as an intervening variable that induces, rather than causes behavior. The offender's decision to choose or accept the inducement for crime establishes an inevitability rationality, but it remains the offender's choice rather than the inducement that establishes this inevitability rationality.

(c) <u>Criminality of the Addictive</u> - This subcategory is usually illustrated by alcoholics and drug addicts. The addict commits crime either to support his habit, particularly the drug addict, or as a result of the substance abuse - the most common examples being the offender who steals to buy drugs and the drunken driver. What is characteristic of this group is their habit of dependence on a substance as a means of dealing with stress, tension or anxiety. With prolonged substance use, greater doses are needed to relieve tension which is increased in the neuro-transmitting, bio-chemical constitution by the substance abuse and dependence.

Medical evidence indicates that since there are identifiable and significant bio-chemical changes in the addict, a disease does, in fact, exist. However, while the addict's perceptions are mandatory in advanced states of addiction, the ability to choose not to be dependent still exists. The offender chooses to allow the perception of mandatory impulse and often fills the impulse with alcohol or drugs, or increasingly, a combination of the two. His rationality is inevitable because he chose to accept what induces inevitability.

(d) <u>Addictive Criminality</u> - An addictive criminal is one addicted to one (or more) of the prior rationalities (and where applicable, the mental-emotional disturbance sub-category of the inevitability rationality) such that over time and with practice it becomes a habit. The offender reasons that his criminal adaptation is inevitably necessary. While a score of 4 on a rationality indicates extreme seriousness, it may or may not also indicate the presence of addictive criminality. The distinguishing factor is the "must be" quality of the rationality. In such a case, the offender, if he were to have a 4 on functional rationality, would also be characterized as having an addictive criminality form of an inevitability rationality which would be listed and scored separately. An addictive, mental-emotional disturbance such as with a persistent sex offender would be similarly listed and scored according to both the disturbance and the addiction as a multi-classification.

METHODOLOGY

After scoring for Bumping and Rationality, the analyst should describe the institutional and field settings for data input and present each case according to the following:

Case Study Reporting

1) Personal and Demographic information: pseudonym, year of birth, sex, race or ethnic group, height, weight, county and state, religion.
2) Offenses (past and present).
3) Presenting problems.
4) Source of referral.
5) School History.
6) Family History.
7) Social History.
8) Classification and scoring - includes any further classifications germane to the offender and illustrates all classification scoring with examples of the offender's behavior. The analyst should include salient feelings, images, emotions and sensations associated with the offender's rationality (lies).
9) Behavior Variables. These variables as with the prior scoring should be illustrated by examples of the offender's behavior. The analyst is also asked to indicate whether legal processing and psychological evaluations have under/over or correctly estimated the reality of the offender s behavior (legal) and mentality (psychological).
10) Treatment Implications - The treatment recommendations should be directed to the problems illustrated in the category, classification and behavior variable accounts so that the bases for the recommendations are documented.
11) Labeling - It is important for all case analysts and participating agency administrators to realize that the conceptual basis of this classification is in total accordance with the principles and implications of reality based behavioral criminological therapies. Numerical ratings are used in order to gener-

ate greater scientific precision in classifying, treating and evaluating the most effective and humane methods of bringing about change from criminogenic behavior and thinking to non-criminogenic behavior and thinking.

At no time should any definitive designation from this cognitive counseling classification (numerical and/or descriptive) be interpreted as a final determinative label of an offender's thinking or behavioral condition. The purpose of this classification is to better identity and understand criminogenic thought and behavior such that we are better able to generate treatment approaches that are more accurate and specific with respect to the potential for change and responsibility in the offender.

To use a metaphor, this classification is a map pointing to directions for change; it is not and cannot be used as a deterministic, behavioralistic or final label.

CHAPTER FOUR

The Criminal Belief Rationality: The Theology of Crime

Introduction

The author presents a "theology of crime" multi-disciplinary analysis applying criminological, historical, psychological and theological references to the study of criminal belief rationalities. The author presents specific case studies along with general policy analysis, including legal analysis, with case specific and general policy recommendations to include a comparative analysis of the KKK (Ku Klux Klan) and the NOI (Nation of Islam). Along with an account of the author's personal observations of and experiences with a "cult modus operandi", the author presents four very different case studies of the varied aspects of the "theology of crime" to include: Dr. Baruch Goldstein, Dr. Josef Mengele, a KKK skinhead, and a violent anti-abortion protestor.

The criminal belief rationality, which I've further qualified as the theology of crime, applies to a variety of belief systems wherein a religious belief in God or a secular belief in a God-like substitute is a major causative factor in criminality.

In illustrating the religious belief rationality in the theology of crime, I shall be presenting the case of Dr. Baruch Goldstein, as a recent example of a religious mass murderer in his crime of the murder of Muslims at prayers in the Cave of the Patriarchs. In illustrating the secular belief rationality, I shall compare the dynamics of what can be similarly identified and compared in the religious belief rationality of Dr. Goldstein and the secular belief rationality of Dr. Josef Mengele, as the angel, or more theologically accurate, devil of death.

Although the scale of criminality in terms of the numbers of victims cannot be equated, and although the belief rationality systems of a Goldstein and Mengele are not only quite distinct and anti-opposite in terms of being at the extremes of opposition to very different particular others and, most particularly, in a very different opposition to each other, there are, nevertheless, similarities in some central constructs of belief rationality. More than one Israeli professor has applied the term "Judeo-Nazi" to the Kach movement that Goldstein belonged to. Such a term has been used to designate a branch of what many Israelis consider "foreign", "settler" Judaism in designating Goldstein's American origins from their own in a brand of hyphenated Nazism.

Due to the similarities even more than the differences between these two distinct but not isolated cases, in being distinct in their unrelated crimes but not isolated in their related rationalities, I shall utilize theological, criminological and historic references to clarify the specifics and to analyze their broader implications.

The two most uncommon cases of Drs. Goldstein and Mengele will be analyzed in reference to the common construct of the theology of crime that they both closely share in common. They will be followed by two far more common cases that have nothing in common according to a religious or secular manifestation of the criminal belief rationality: the first case being that of a Ku Klux Klan skinhead, and the second being that of a violent anti-abortion protestor. I will also be presenting an account of the "cult modus operandi" from my personal observation of and experience with common cult practices, along with my analysis of militant cults to include an analysis of the KKK (Ku Klux Klan) and the NOI (Nation of Islam) in reference to each other.

Recommendations will be presented throughout as to how to best treat worst case scenarios like those presented with treatment being defined as cognitive treatment in attempting to change one's cognitive process associated with a criminal belief rationality ... before it reaches the final solution of finalizing others as a solution.

This rationality is to be distinguished from the plethora of criminal cases that reveal a precipient mental and/or emotional disturbance expressed in terms of a belief system. Such cases to be excluded from cognitive belief rationality would be those of "The Devil Made Me Do It" or "God Told Me To Do It" varieties. These kinds of cases are excluded because even though some of the theological references or religious catch words, or Kach words, may sound similar or may even be the same, the cognitive rationality is quite different.

There is a distinct cognitive demarcation between a person who believes in the commandments of Moses or the teachings of Jesus and one who accepts the idea of God or Satan, and someone who thinks he is Moses or Jesus or God or Satan. Similarly, there is a clear cognitive difference between a believer who listens to the Word of the Lord, for example, and someone who hears words from the Lord telling him to break the law.

On a related note, I would mention the large number of cases of those who've personally "gotten the word" from the Lord as distinct from those who personally know "The Word of the Lord", in the exceptionally high number of the emotionally disturbed referring to themselves as Jesus. In this regard, I recall a comment from a recently deceased professor of criminology, a Jewish friend and colleague, who confided in me that he'd much prefer hearing someone assert he's Jesus, than hearing him claim that he's Adolph Hitler.

With these qualifications and comments in mind, one can observe that in our American culture of religious pluralism and secular freedom, the relationship between religion and crime has been relegated to an analytic cult status. The idea that one can be turned away from crime by "getting religion" has been extensively preached and occasionally practiced, just as the idea that religion can be a criminological turn on, as well as a turn off, has been extensively ignored in both religious and secular quarters.

Most of the world's religions - mainline and marginal - have a history of not only saints but sinners ... to include sinners whose sins are crimes. Just as there's a widely documented Psychology of Crime and Sociology of Crime and Ecology of Crime among other social scientific studies of crime, there exists a Theology of Crime, as well, although it has not been documented as such.

Dr. Baruch Goldstein, the Doctor of religious murder, in committing the horrid crime of the mass murder of Muslims at prayer in the Cave of the Patriarchs, was a unique example of the theology of crime, although this "very religious" Jewish mass murderer is in no way unique in the long history of "very religious" Christians and Muslims, among others, who've committed murder in the name of their religious theology.

Goldstein's religious criminality and criminal rationality of a theology of divine hate is not unique, nor unfortunately, is its horror confined to his crime, for as unbelievable as it may sound (for those who believe that religion and crime should be incompatible) there were eulogies in his honor by some "very religious" voices from his Kach Party to include a rabbi's voice, whose invocation of their "holy man of God" confirmed their Nazi Kach-up criminality in catching up to Nazi-like hate.

The particular case of a Dr. Goldstein, as unique as it may appear, is illustrative of what is both general and particular in the theology of crime as the study of the God of crime, of a criminal God of divine hate. There's a tendency to relegate religious inspired criminality to cult status because cultists tend to be more extreme and, therefore, they're more likely to be deviant in a variety of ways and, sometimes, more suicidal.

The author is personally familiar with cults, in having experienced a common manipulative "cult modus operandi" that is as typical among cults as their belief systems can be atypical: which experiences will be presented along with the aforementioned case studies.

However while the theology of crime can be a disreputable, marginal and sometimes suicidal phenomenon, as evidenced in Jim Jones and the Peoples Temple, and in David Koresh and the Branch Davidians among others, it can also be a mainline and sometime homicidal aspect of reputable, in terms of non-deviant religion.

One can easily document the religious criminality of the theology of crime and the criminal religiosity of divine hate in the historical criminal rap-sheet of Judaism, Christianity and Islam from the Biblical Hebrew invocation to slay men, women and children, to the unholy Office of the Catholic Inquisition, to the Islamic Jihad, to Protestant crimes against other Protestants who protested too much against established Protestantism, right up to the present day Islamic Hamas, the "God Gave Your Land To Me" religious cleansing of Nazi-like Kach-ups, the Orthodox blessing of Serbian ethnic cleansing, and Christian fundamentalist inspired abortion clinic bombings and murder

I believe that the legal psychology of hate laws in "hating hate" in legalizing correctness is not only bad psychology, but also bad law. It is more likely to increase, psychologically, what it attempts to correct, legally, with the quite incorrect censorship of correctness. Nevertheless, there is a need, a dire need, to determine what truly is correct, in policy and procedure, in dealing with the theology of crime.

Before attempting to make any recommendations for dealing with the varied criminogenic beliefs of criminal belief rationalities in a society wherein the very notion of a "theology of crime" criminality is regarded by many as an unconscionable sin against an unconstitutional religious and secular correctness, one must establish the broad parameters of a social psychological critique that incorporates both secular and religious analyses.

In the United States, the most spectacular illustrations of the criminal belief rationality in recent memory have been seen in cults such as Jim Jones' Peoples Temple and the Branch Davidians with David Koresh as their self-described "criminal" Messiah. The religious pluralism of America, as attractively free as it may be in promoting its constitutional freedom of religion, nevertheless, has produced radically free constitutionals of religious free radicals, in a most unattractive religious environment of a bizarre assortment of criminally terminal cults and sects. Not a few of them engage in crime and many more of them display a strong criminal tendency.

European observers have been prone to point in disbelief at the incredible assortment of incredulous belief systems freely at work in the United States, with observations to the effect that "only in America," as "the land of opportunity," is there every opportunity for a church for every belief and a belief for every church. While that less than complementary appraisal has been and still is accurate, this religious situation of "a belief in any belief" is by no means limited to the United States, as the recent case of The Order of the Solar Temple with its Canadian and European membership indicates.

The American comedian, Joan Rivers, once commented that only in California can one find "Nazi Quakers". As funny as that may sound, at least to some Californians, that "California dreamin" spirit of anything goes regarding just about any belief is no longer confined to California or America. There appears to be an increasing spirit of deregulatory spiritual freedom that has little to do with what's traditionally regulated by the Holy Spirit, and it has much to do with a "Freedom in the Spirit" to be free in any way in any spirit.

In conversations with cult members I have encountered very few who have any substantial theological training in being able to analyze and distinguish belief systems, let alone to apply even a recognizable minimal theological standard of evaluation or judgement. While the Jesuit definition of faith is that of "an intellectual assent of the will", the cult definition is more an anti-intellectual assent of the will... in replacing an intellectual faith with an irrational will. The common cult reaction is a programmed one of being either "in" or "out", "for" or "against"... in being more "of the compound of their world" than "of the kingdom that is not of this world."

While they often refer to their "sacred" freedom of religion to believe and to do whatever their belief frees them to do - to themselves or others - there is hardly any freedom left for anything or anyone else. This abhorrence of any freedom other than their own total freedom - in total indulgences and dispensations - is evidenced in blanket denunciations of opposing opinions that are often characterized as being those of a "Great Satan" or some other evil source

Among the cult leadership in general, one can observe power oriented personalities with the desire to control others by dispensing punishments and rewards; while among the cult membership, one observes personalities who need to belong and to be accepted. What often appears most incongruous, at first, among cult members is the fact that some of them not only come from well-to-do middle class backgrounds, but some have attained surprisingly high levels of education. One of the Branch Davidians, for example, was a graduate of the Harvard Law School. What this apparent incongruity demonstrates is that in the area of belief rationalities, one's emotional needs are capable of overriding one's mental abilities.

The need to be accepted, in effect, to be given an unconditional acceptance equivalent to that which a child should get from a loving family, but which fewer children seem to be getting from more single parent to no-parent American families, can be seen among cult members in need of a family substitute. The absence of primal family nurturing in the backgrounds of many cult members explains much of the primal irrationality of their adherence to a cult belief rationality.

In order to illustrate this point further, I'll relate an incident which I experienced while waiting for a flight at the Denver airport terminal. I had a two hour delay and while sitting alone - and undoubtedly looking conspicuously lonely - I was approached by a young woman who asked me if I wouldn't mind talking with her for a while. Since she appeared to be exceptionally attractive and wholesome looking, I replied "How could I possibly mind?" In a matter of minutes, the conversation turned to spiritual matters, such as how to be really happy with God and how her particular "spiritual family" had a special relationship with God. Before I knew it, I was joined by three others (two women and a man), who offered me flowers and candy.

To make a long story short, after two hours of conversation during which time I thoroughly enjoyed some more flowers and candy, and during which time I never indicated any disinclination to believe or reluctance to go along with what they were saying, I was ready to board my plane. As I stood up and prepared to bid them a pleasant good-bye, the young woman who'd first approached me asked me to give her my address and phone numbers so that "the family" could contact me. Further, she and the other family members pressed on with further family contact in the form of actual physical contact – to the point of physically pressing against me – in trying to impress upon me, literally, how much "they loved me".

Being somewhat of a cantankerous soul, I couldn't resist the opportunity to continue to go along with their programmed program... in going along with their literal impressions. After a few moments of what appeared to be a family reunion of sorts in "the family's" sordid emotional pretense of a normal family's emotions, I announced to them that I, too, had something very much in common with them. Having intensified their expectation of having made another recruit in another "made family member," I stated, "You know, I love myself, too... Goodbye!"

Not unsurprisingly, their unqualified expression of love quickly turned to surprise as it more slowly turned into the expression of an unqualified quality of hate... as I scurried off to the non-loving but familiar embrace of my compressed seat in the economy section of the airplane.

The point of this story, as unreal as it may sound in its cultish dialogue, is the very real emotionally manipulative strategies of cults that often rely in no small measure in impressing one with all the emotional supports of a family - with the initial impression of a measure of supporting sex.

Once one joins a cult "family" one is either put to work or made to pay for the continued love and acceptance of the parental-control figures - in one way or another - upon whom one is made to feel dependent... in every possible conceivable emotional way.

In discussions with cult believers, some of whom, unbelievable as it may seem, seem to be quite intelligent, articulate and reasonable, I noticed what I describe as a "bracketing personality". This type of personality can intelligently and normally interact with other people in most respects with the one exception of whatever questions the central belief components of the cult... which beliefs are protected by mental and emotional bracketing.

When one questions their belief system as a newcomer or outsider in a general inquiring way that denotes a potential convert, their responses are quite rational, controlled and even professional. However, should one display an inquisitive persistence that goes beyond asking questions to questioning answers, the reaction is that of a bracketed mental and emotional "shut-down", wherein the belief system is protected by being totally bracketed so as to escape any scrutiny.

In a dramatically demonstrable and very observable manner, the cult believer will "shut-down" not only the conversation but, also, his personality and your person... so that there is no further possibility of discussion or questioning. In so bracketing one's belief system, one isolates the central believing aspect of one's self from not only one's intellect, but from one's normal personality.

On more than one occasion I've observed what I metaphorize as a "trap door" simultaneously shutting down both the mind and the personality whenever the believer feels trapped by any open crack in the closed door of his crackpot belief. This bracketing personality process explains how a seemingly intelligent and well educated person functions within a cult. Very simply, his or her intelligence and education is bracketed and replaced by his emotionally dependent and addictive belief system when the belief is challenged. When the challenge recedes, the normal personality reappears as quickly as it disappeared... in a metaphor of a revolving door of a bracketed open-closed door personality.

In attempting to criminally categorize cults, one can only say that they cover the entire range of the Penal Code from a lack of hesitation to commit the most serious crimes against an enemy (most often characterized as a Satanic enemy) to passive cults who are content with limiting their exploitation to the passive receptivity of their members.

A very specialized and highly dangerous criminality can be attributed to the militant religious defense leagues, as being comprised of some of the most aggressive and violent criminals who thrive on appropriating - or more accurately misappropriating - the names of the Islamic, Jewish and Christian religions to themselves. In addition to the Islamic Hamas and Jihad Party of God terrorists, and the Jewish Defense League and Kach Party terrorists, there are the old and new Christian Identity KKK - related criminals... with a most peculiar anti-Christian proclivity for burning crosses in terrorizing anyone with a different identity than their own.

With the economic fallout of the falling away of the national economic infrastructure in out-contracting to cheaper labor abroad, in importing cheaper labor at home, one can expect major personality dislocations to accompany economic dislocations. The predictable consequence of the economic machinations of a GATT global free trade "harmonized" world economy will be quite the opposite of harmonious for the have-nots, in a divisive economic class system best characterized by that old Afro-American adage of "Them that gots gets".

The North American know-how of the how-to pace setter of a NAFTA -

know how to - SHAFTA has already helped set the pace for a resurgence of a very different know-how in the how to hate knowledge of America's Know Nothings. The old American KKK know-how, however, can adjust itself in a heartbeat to the pulse beat of changing circumstances in monitoring its own pulse, in setting a new pace in a pulsating know-nothingness of knowing how to beat up on others.

At one time, the KKK so-called white Christian warriors would make the most unpleasant house calls on many Black people, a few Brown people, fewer Yellow people, (simply because there were fewer of them), and even fewer Red people (now known as Native Americans) who were the fewest of all in the few survivors of America's Holocaust against the only Americans who were native to America. In addition to racial animus, the KKK was also an equal opportunity, affirmative action hater, in taking every opportunity to affirm and act on hate. Jews, in particular, followed by Catholics - most particularly of the Irish immigrant and southern European stock - were hated for being outside of a real, white, Protestant American right kind of stock.

However, to give the Devil his due, if you'll excuse the cultist phraseology, the KKK has adapted itself to changing circumstances without changing its racial adaptation. In adjusting to the substantial growth of a Catholic population comprising approximately 25% of the American population, "appropriate" Catholics are now not only no longer enemies but potential friends. An "appropriate" Catholic, for those not accustomed to KKK correctness, is a white, preferably Northern European Catholic of Irish, German, Ukrainian, Polish or Lithuanian descent, to exclude Hispanics and Asians, of course.

A recent example of this adaptation occurred at a cemetery desecration in a Western state, wherein Jewish tombstones were overturned and defaced while Catholic tombstones were untouched. As economic tensions drive racial tensions, there's a strong probability that the KKK will succeed in further recruiting disaffected economically disadvantaged Catholics to their white robed apparel. The Catholic Church has and will continue to strongly oppose such a development, but economic non-developments, unfortunately, are likely to prove stronger than any church developments in this area.

Stalin once asked, "How many divisions does the Pope have?"; whereas today, one might ask, "How many jobs does the Church have to offset the NAFTA-SHAFTA exportation of North America's manufacturing base south of the border?"

The following case of Matt, a teenage KKK skinhead, is a recent illustration of what is both new and old in this kind of criminal belief rationality. In presenting this case, I shall quote directly from the youth's case file... while keeping his identity confidential. The report of Matt's high school friend reads as follows:

"I first met Matt in the fall of my freshman year of high school and stayed in contact with him until May of 1994. Matt came from a troubled home, his father had just lost his job at a factory near our homes.

He blamed this on the insurgence of minorities into the area, but the real reason was his father's drinking problems. Matt's father had been in the KKK most of his adult life and Matt grew up with these views. During our early years of high school Matt had always been in trouble mostly to gain the attention of his father. In September of our junior year he joined a local group of skinheads that had just appeared in our area and became very active with them. This is when he started getting into real trouble with the law. His first major arrest was for aggravated assault, this took place at a local concert. Matt and a group of his friends beat up a young black man and put him in the hospital. He was able to plead out of this because he was a minor. From then on he was always in some kind of trouble. He was arrested for simple assault, assault and battery, breaking and entering, and, later, for murder. Throughout this time he was strongly involved in the skinheads. He really believed that the minorities in our community were the reason for both his and his father's problems."

Matt often expressed the belief that his criminal activity would help the people he cared about... the white race. He felt that the only way the white race could end its repression was through violence. Being a member of a skinhead group was very important to him; and he openly expressed his pride of membership in tattooing his body with Aryan supremacy and KKK symbols. His case report continues:

"Matt believed that his father had lost his job because of the minorities in the community. He also thought that they were going to bring the rest of the community down to their level. The Jews were another group that he thought were trying to hurt his race. He believed that they were trying to control finance and that they would eventually own everything."

The group that Matt belonged to strongly opposed drugs in maintaining that it was a means to hold the white race back. Obviously, just saying no to drugs doesn't say much about what one might say yes to. Unfortunately, if not ironically, one has to acknowledge that some of the most effective anti-drug influence among youths - white and black - has been exerted by the most extreme racist elements at the KKK (Ku Klux Klan) and NOI (Nation of Islam) fringes of their respective white and black communities.

In theological analysis, a heresy has been defined as the overemphasis of a forgotten truth. In this mutual KKK and NOI racial heresy of mutual racism, one must publicly assert that the correct emphasis upon their anti-drug truth cannot be based on forgetting the lie of one's own racism in remembering the ugly truth of others racism. The "Black is Beautiful" emphasis on one's own race that becomes a less than beautiful "white is ugly" is as wrong as a "white is right" racism. Such racism needs to be defined as an overemphasis of one forgotten truth in forgetting another truth that any racism - be it proactively white or reactively black - is always a lie. The lie of racism should be presented and taught in our schools as a moral weakness and amoral addiction that weakens one's race.

Throughout Matt's delinquent career in careening towards a full-fledged criminality, he'd experienced many contacts with the juvenile justice system. Rather than helping him or deterring him, such contacts seemed to encourage his progressive criminality in further reinforcing his already reinforced belief that whatever he did... the revolving door of the justice system would keep turning. Finally, after being convicted of murder, he discovered that the revolving door wouldn't be turning him around that easily... in having to wait somewhat longer for another turn until his 25 year sentence of hard prison time has been completed.

To the extreme degree that Matt represents the criminal belief rationality of the non-forgotten heresy of an all too well remembered racism, the following case of Frank represents another extreme belief in the extreme degree to which a "true believer" might go in opposing abortion as a sin worse than any heresy... or death.

Frank, a twenty-five year old white male from a large Roman Catholic family, had been very active in his community and church since day one. Prior to getting involved with anti-abortion protests, he had been a very popular youth sports coach. His presenting problems with the justice system had all resulted from anti-abortion protests culminating in three arrests for disorderly conduct and one arrest for criminal trespass.

As evidenced in most of the anti-abortion protestors who tend to be devout believers in a fundamentalist version of either Biblical Protestantism or Traditionalist Catholicism, or sometimes in both, Frank had displayed a proclivity to believe everything he'd been taught in the name of religion - to include every dogmatic dot on every theological doctrine - with no room for compromise with any other or, especially, any middle way.

In what I'd describe as an "Infallible Psychology of Faith," Frank displayed a very common rationality in this group, what I term "a holistic psychoholy of holy faith" in what I further describe as "a Psychoholy of Crime." This belief rationality totally negates the justice system with the total justification of a totalitarian faith... one that affirms its holiness in totally ruling out any other faith. Its modus operandi is that of an operational infallibility as to a particular matter of holy dispute...in this case, the medical operation of abortion.

In analyzing this kind of psychoholic offender, there are both similarities and differences with the aforementioned cult offenders and with the militant religious defense leagues. Like the cult offenders, there's a certain bracketing of the personality in refusing to admit, acknowledge or allow for the possibility of error, which is equated with disbelief; and like the militant religious defense leagues, there's no reluctance to use aggression and violence as "defenders of the faith".

The violent abortion protestor, however, is distinguished from the cult believer in being able to ground his criminal rationality in a respectable traditional, and orthodox religious theology. Such traditional religious grounding makes his position appear to be all the more legitimate and morally righteous (to himself and others) - in being truly more holy in more holy truth. Any differing position is regarded as being that of an unholy liberal deviance proceeding from a very wrong situational ethics and amoral relative morality.

Although the overwhelming majority of Catholics and Protestants, to include traditionalists and fundamentalists among them, eschew any form of violence, aggression or criminality in protesting abortion, there exists a theological inducement for criminality in the "psychoholic rhetoric" of the anti-abortion movement. Quite simply, terminology that equates abortion with the Nazi Holocaust and describes doctors who perform abortion as "child murderers" establishes a "psychoholic justification" for the ultimate in violence... in the ultimate irony of Pro Life becoming pro taking of life to save life.

The majority of Americans, consisting of a Protestant and Catholic citizens, have expressed a middle ground Roe v. Wade consensus on abortion that distances itself from the extremes of both the pro-choice and pro-life movements. While Catholic doctrine is more absolutist on abortion than main line Protestantism, the anti-abortion movement cannot be characterized in terms of any one religious denomination. Although religious infallibility is associated with Papal infallibility, Catholic doctrine applies infallibility only in the most rare and limited of circumstances, wherein the Pope speaks "ex cathedra" or "from the chair" on a binding matter of faith or morals. As contrasted to the fundamentalist Protestant doctrine of Biblical inerrancy wherein every word in the Bible is to be taken literally, at every time and at every occasion, the Catholic traditionalist penchant for religious extremism is far less pervasive than that of Protestant fundamentalism.

On the issue of abortion, however, the two historic extremes reflected in modern Protestant and Catholic extremism, which have been at odds with each other in the past over theological literalism, to the literal degree of engaging in religious wars against one another, have now combined forces in a concerted holy war. No longer is God on one side only, for God has now embraced both sides to the new ecumenical tune of an infallible - inerrant religious concert that wails away at the heathen at the wall - a heathen being anyone who allows for abortion.

Rather than describing the movement as Catholic or fundamentalist Protestant, it can more accurately be described as a religious extremism that provides a "psychoholic legitimacy" for a psychologically illegitimate "Infallible Psychology of Faith".

In attempting to psychoanalyze faith, one might best utilize the Jesuit definition of faith "as the intellectual assent of the will". This intellectual definition of what begins with but doesn't end with one's intellect can be supplemented by more emotive and less intellectual definitions such as that which goes beyond reason and intellect to "seeing the invisible, believing the incredible and receiving the impossible".

There are times such as the present, however, which not only try men's souls but try their minds. Foremost among them, the rational religious minds, in a multiplicitude of faiths that not only "surpass human understanding", but that go much further into the irrational beyond a reasonable faith to a faith in the irrational... in surpassing the understanding of the moral absolutes of a rational faith with the moral misunderstanding of an absolute irrationality.

Violent abortion protestors such as Frank display a clear and evident need for an irrational "psychoholic infallibility" that reflects a pathology of both faith and reason. In hiding what's all-too-fallible in themselves behind a "psychoholic breastplate of righteousness", one observes the classic urge to punish others in order to retain absolute certainty for their all-too-errant selves.

While Americans are guaranteed their First Amendment freedom of religion - which freedom as with any freedom, is only free when it's free enough to tolerate the (non-criminal) abuse of freedom - I would recommend that all religious education of an absolutist nature should amend itself, first, in upholding the absolute freedom of others to hold a different position.

In comparing Catholics and Protestants on making the intellectual and moral distinction between "a matter of faith" and "a matter of intellect", I've observed that traditionalist Catholics, who hold the same absolute position as fundamentalist Protestants, are more likely to respond to such a distinction. That doesn't mean that Catholics are more likely to change their minds about their faith; but it does mean that they are more likely to be of a different mind in imposing their faith on others.

The reason for this distinctive difference between anti-abortionists of a traditionalist Catholic persuasion and those of a fundamentalist Protestant persuasion is not one of a greater or lesser reason or faith, but, rather, one of a different notion as to differing persuasions. Catholics do not differ greatly from Protestants in their religious persuasion, but they do differ in their very different experience of being a religious minority. Catholics, who migrated to a Protestant America as a poor, initially despised "No Irish Need Apply" Papist, supposedly anti-democratic ethnic - religious groups - despite the leadership, particularly of the Irish, in establishing unions and the Democratic Party - were forced to acculturate as a minority in outwardly and publicly conforming to what they inwardly and privately might believe to the contrary.

This experience of the political necessity for adaptive compromise - most of all moral compromise - was a very positive one in experiencing the need for necessary adaptation in the deadly arena of moral political conflict. This need, which is needed now more than ever, is one that Catholic ethnics relate to far more readily than Protestant nativists of Anglo-Saxon and Scottish-Irish fundamentalist background.

While it might be quite fine to repeat with Patrick Henry, "Give Me Liberty or Give Me Death", today's moral refrains are not quite so fine in a "Give Me My Liberty To My Right To Enforce What's Right or Give Me Death... Your Death."

Whereas the criminal cult belief rationality manifests itself in the "bracketed personality," the extreme religious belief rationality exemplified in the violent abortion protestor suspends the personality in the suspended psychoholic animation of "the infallible psychology of faith." Such a personality is also bracketed; but it displays the further characteristic of drawing upon a respectable non-deviant religious tradition in a most righteous "psychoholic personality" - albeit a bracketed one of a justified infallibility that overrides a fallible justice system... one that animates itself in the irrational mental suspension of an infallible faith in its justifications by its faith alone.

While many religious rationalities can be extreme, not all are criminal. What distinguishes a faith that supplements reason from one that contradicts reason in going beyond a rational faith to criminally acting upon a faith in the irrational, is that which distinguishes a law abiding religious belief from a criminal belief in the name of religion.

It's quite true that some of the violence of the abortion protestors may be attributed to mental or emotional disturbance in some offenders seeking a "hyper-religious notoriety" which is quite different from the common copy-cat criminality in terms of its modus vivendi, but which is quite similar in terms of its modus operandi in seeking recognition. Nevertheless, the essence of this criminal belief rationality cannot be characterized according to mental-emotional pathology or common criminality. However disturbing the irrationality of the belief system may appear to be, there is a criminal rationality that is not disturbed, in being in complete control of itself. The rationality is one that employs religion for the intent of crime in a disturbingly calculated but non-disturbed and reasoned (if not rational) manner that constitutes legal men's reason... the intent to commit the act... albeit with a reasoned infallibility that not only surpasses but appears to contradict the notion or, rather, our notion of reason.

In an explicitly demonstrable fashion, the choice of criminality is made and justified by a distortion of rational religious reasoning in a "psychoholic", irrational, "infallible psychology of faith."

In attempting to counter religious irrationality one must rely on religious reason due to the fact that secular reasoning, alone, will be dismissed in being bracketed out as being out of the faith, in being "Not of the Lord." It is significant to note in this respect that the most successful incident in negotiating with hostage-taking Islamic terrorists occurred at the Algiers airport when a negotiator quoted the Koran to the terrorists in successfully convincing them to release their hostages.

I strongly believe that if the American government negotiators at the Branch Davidian compound in Waco, Texas, had a better understanding of belief rationality and, therefore, a better strategy for responding to David Koresh's Bible quoting references to the seventh seal, at least the children in the compound might have been saved. Traditional hostage negotiation techniques for dealing with common criminals or political ideologues are quite inappropriate for dealing with extremists motivated by a belief rationality.

In negotiating with a violent anti-abortion protestor with a background similar to that of Frank, for example, a Catholic priest would be far more effective than a government official or someone from Planned Parenthood. Similarly, in dealing with a potential Baruch Goldstein, a rabbi with a deep understanding of Goldstein's orthodox theology stands a far greater chance of success than a Prime Minister Rabin. As in the Islamic terrorist incident at the Algiers airport, an appropriately trained negotiator, with detailed knowledge of the belief rationality in evidence is worth all of the FBI, ATF and Justice Dept. officials put together, to include their behavioral science division, in negotiating with a Bible quoting fanatic.

The area of the most extreme and uncompromising violence in the name of religion can be observed in the militant religious defense leagues. While the majority of Islamic and Jewish Defense League terrorism (more appropriately described as Religious Terrorist Offense Leagues) reflects the Arab-Israeli and Jewish-Muslim conflicts in the Middle East, the Nation of Islam (NOI) is an indigenous Black Islamic phenomenon in the United States.

It is no small irony that the Nation of Islam in targeting Jews, as their major white oppressors, in their anti-Jewish sermons accompanied by a few aspersions of an anti-Catholic nature (such as the reference to the Pope as that "no-good, old, cracker") strongly resemble the historic enemy of the Black people: the Ku Klux Klan. Ironically, the KKK also targeted Jews as their major (non-white) aggressor (in attacking them not only because of their non-Christian identity but, also, excluding them from a white racial identity), followed by Catholics (some of whom were white but all of whom threatened to take over Protestant America) along with the less than white Southern European immigrants and non-white Hispanics and Orientals (who threatened to pollute white Christian racial purity).

The inverted similarity between the hit lists of the KKK and the NOI is striking in striking out at similar others. All one need do is remove Blacks from the KKK hit list and whites (to exclude Jews) from the NOI hit list, and one would find a similar list of targets to be hit by both groups.

As similar as these racist groups are in their motivational origins of a belief system of aggressive racism, there are, nevertheless, distinct dissimilarities between them in their original motivations. The NOI can be described as an extreme outgrowth of a defensive "Black is Beautiful" counterculture to an offensive "White as Ice-Cold Ugly" and "Jew as Swine" culture of hate. The established press tends to downplay and underestimate the strong appeal and growing popularity of the NOI among many Blacks - to include many well educated Blacks. Furthermore, I see nothing that indicates a decrease in their influence and much that portends an increase in their power... despite the fact that they will be increasingly ignored by Middle America.

One of the reasons for their appeal in the Black community, and one that is no small reason, is their strong presence and highly disciplined activity in crime control: in providing housing project security, community corrections and drug control and delinquency intervention. The NOI is highly respected in their communities because they are "of" and "from" those communities, and further, they provide a belief system with a discipline and structure that is not evident elsewhere. The "Black Gospel" churches also have a strong historic presence, but their image is often that of a "Reverend Ike" and "Brother Love" soft Christianity that is more suited for preparing more Aretha Franklins for Motown fame than for dealing with the infamous problems of a crime-ridden community.

Quite clearly, the NOI is the only clear alternative, at present, in providing an alternative solution with sorely needed discipline, structure and community crime response: most of all community crime control.

In observing a variety of government sponsored welfare and community development initiatives, I observed the tendency to ignore and the attempt to isolate the NOI. I believe that this strategy is wrong for two reasons: one, it won't work and, two, it will actually increase what it hopes to decrease. The NOI is not going to disappear and a strategy of isolating the NOI will only increase its self-isolating extremism, so as to increase its influence in generating more hostility in its becoming less isolated among those who are extremely vulnerable - young, poor, Black males.

Rather than isolation, attempts at incorporating the positive (anti-crime) influences of the NOI, while distancing others (to include NOI members) from certain negative (racist) influences, would be a better strategy. Most attempts to help, most of all the social welfare model of the helping professions, have been mostly less than helpful. Government welfare has not fared well, in failing not only the government that has dispensed welfare but, most of all, in failing the community where welfare has been most dispensed. In fact, the biggest joke in the Black community is the "do-gooder" white social worker who's looked upon as "no-good" in being "good for nothing" other than for conning. In a number of major urban areas I've noticed a preponderance of white social workers of Jewish and Catholic backgrounds that, I feel, is somewhat related to the anti-Jewish and anti-Catholic rhetoric of some, but not all, of the NOI.

There have been some initial steps in the direction of conflict resolution with the NOI that could succeed, I believe, if they were continued and taken further. In particular, a few Catholic clergy in inner city areas have reached out and invited NOI ministers to visit their churches. This kind of inclusive reaching out is recommended over the exclusionary strategy that will produce more harm than good in shutting out (but not shutting down) the NOI.

There are also others "in" and "of" the Black community, such as the Prince Hall Masons, who represent a truly inclusive ecumenical belief system that has tremendous potential for serving as an intermediary in modifying the reactive negatives of some segments of the NOI. Further, Prince Hall Masonry, which is historically rooted in the Black community, is related to the Freemasons, who comprise the oldest and largest fraternity in the world with a belief system based on "The Fatherhood of God and Brotherhood of Man".

In this regard, I've made a number of published recommendations as to the unactivated potential of Freemasonry in helping to overcome the racial, religious and secular ethnocentricity of criminal belief systems (Ryan 1994).

In dealing with KKK related aggressive beliefs, I do feel that the exclusionary policy is the only feasible strategy, since the potential for modifying their belief system by incorporating them into the system does not, in my opinion, exist. The distinctive difference in the belief systems of the NOI and KKK, the one that underlies their surface similarities of racism, is a difference, literally, that is a Black and White difference. The difference in the motivational origins of their similar sounding but quite distinctive racisms is the NOI's original motivation of reacting to white rejection with Black rejection, in rejecting their rejecters in reacting to white hate with Black hate to being excluded by others... while the KKK acts with hate to others being included.

In my opinion, as the NOI is included, the hate driven aspects of their ideology will drive away by themselves, whereas there's no way to drive away the hate ideology of the KKK. To put it in another way, the NOI's system of belief is reactive and it can be changed by the actions of a system that promotes equality (without promoting the inequality of affirmative action). The KKK, on the other hand, is proactive in their belief system beginning and ending with the promotion of hate... with no prospect for any change in their belief.

In returning to the introductory case of Dr. Baruch Goldstein in concluding the long history of the theology of crime, one can see the proactive similarity of a Goldstein's Kach-up Judeo-Nazism (as Israeli academics, themselves, have described it) to the proactive criminality of the KKK. There is a major difference, nevertheless, in that unlike the educationally limited and economically disadvantaged KKK skinhead offender like Matt, Goldstein is far more like another doctor, the Nazi Doctor Josef Mengele, in his higher level of education and intelligence.

As simple as the KKK skinhead case of Matt and the violent abortion protestor case of Frank are in terms of traditional analysis, the cases of the Judeo-Nazi

Doctor and the German-Nazi Doctor are complex. They are complex because they blend good and evil, the expected and the unexpected, the admirable and the despicable, the laudable and the unspeakable, in combining the profession of healing and professed destruction in one professional person.

Prior to Nazi criminality, highly educated and intelligent professionals, particularly medical professions, were hardly ever studied in terms of criminological analysis - in a secular humanistic assumption as to the moral superiority of the God of Science and Reason. Similarly, a highly religious person, particularly a religious Jew such as Goldstein, was more likely to be criminologically considered in terms of victimology, of being a likely victim of crime rather than a likely victimizer - in a religious assumption of a Judeo-Christian "chosen" inheritance of Godly virtue.

The unique criminality of Nazism, in its unique evil compounding its unique crimes, engendered unique challenges to a variety of psychological, criminological, humanistic and religious assumptions. Preconceptions were challenged and continue to be challenged, as they should be, as legal assumptions based upon First Amendment freedoms are also being challenged, as they should not be, according to the new challenge to freedom in what's known as "correctness" - in attempting to correct freedom by incorrectly amending freedom.

In spite of and because of our cherished freedom of religion (which must be cherished) and our Constitutional freedom of speech and expression (which is only free when it's free enough to tolerate the abuse of that freedom) there needs to be a criminological determination as to what is not correct in religion. A correct criminological determination, however, should not be confused with correctness - which legislates the freedom to be hatefully wrong or worse, to be right, in being wrongly right in being hatefully right. Correctness infringes upon freedom, as bad laws proceed from bad cases, in criminalizing incorrect, wrong or hateful expression, in the hateful mistake that hate laws take in taking away freedom in the incorrectness of political or religious correctness.

Therefore, despite the serious and unaddressed problem that the theology of crime presents in both its reputable and disreputable religious manifestations, the easy and sinful temptations to ban a sinful holy man, or burn a hateful holy book, or outlaw an outside of the law cult, is wholly wrong. It's wrong because correctness is not correct in that what is corrected may be incorrect only in violating correctness, and what is popularly wrong or politically incorrect may be personally right or singularly correct.

Correctness is based on the socialization of truth which impoverishes truth as much as socialism impoverishes people.

Nevertheless, in refusing to limit freedom in reaction to the abuse of freedom in the further abuse of correctness, the need to establish a standard for distinguishing what is not correct in the religious rationalization that functions as a divine rationality for the theology of crime remains. Further, the implementation of that standard, in respect for freedom of speech and religion, needs to be applied internally within religion rather than imposed externally upon it.

Censor Emptor, let the censor beware, in being aware that do-good censorship does freedom no good; and Censored Emptor, let the self-censored beware, that religious censorship in the name of God or censorship of religion in the name of Man, does God or Man no good.

Therefore, in any criminological approach to correcting the theology of crime, a correct choice is called for - a spiritual choice that looks inward in correcting itself rather than outward in correcting others.

Just as there is correct and incorrect science, there is correct and incorrect religion in terms of "getting religion" in correcting crime or causing crime. The criminological analysis of the theology of crime in rehabilitating in getting religion has to incorporate rehabilitation in getting away from the religious crime of the theology of divine hate: defined as any theology that appropriates a divine or divine substitute for the purpose of hate.

The immediate educational issue is that of how to treat the criminality of divine hate rather than attempt to censor it, and to determine if there has been even one successful precedent.

Believe it or not, to those who are true believers who'd like to truly believe, and to those who are true unbelievers - in having no faith in the criminological prospect of treating religious crime - the most holy task of criminal rehabilitation can work even if it isn't written in any holy book.

In any criminological treatment plan, however, the diagnosis of the cause of the problem constitutes 90% of the cure. Therefore the cause of the theology of crime, that of transcendent choice, needs to be clearly diagnosed.

A correct religious choice, be it that of a Christian choice for God in Jesus, an Islamic choice of God's Messenger, the Prophet Muhammed, or the Enlightened choice in the Way of Enlightment of the Buddha, is that of universal spiritual chosenness wherein God is equally chosen by and for all men and women.

An incorrect religious choice in producing religious criminality is a criminal religiosity wherein chosenness becomes chosinness - a sinful choice - a term I've chosen to designate self-serving, religious group chosinness as contrasted to other-serving, universal spiritual chosenness.

Furthermore, a chosin theological choice is a criminal sinful choice in the crime of sinning against others and in the sin of crime against others - which sinful crime and criminal sin can occur secularly as well as religiously. It occurs in the religious chosinness of one transcendent God as one's God in transcending over and against others; and it occurs secularly in the secular chosinness of putting oneself (and/or one's group) in the place of one God in displacing God in the self-serving place of one's secular transcendence without the Transcendent.

The Hitlerian refrain of "Ein Volk, Ein Reich, Ein Fuehrer" (One People,

One Realm, One Leader) was the ultimate example of this transcendent secular process of chosinness (wherein the idea of chosenness and a Chosen People was used for the idea of a new Chosen People - the Master Race). This Master secular cleansing adaptation of religious cleansing was the concentration camp parent of ethnic cleansing and a close cousin of religious cleansing. It was one that proceeded from its own secular transcendent version of chosenness: a religious cleansing wherein the religious concept of a Chosen People became that of a Chosin People - a People of Sin - when the new Chosen People, the Master Race, appropriated chosenness to themselves in eliminating the Chosen People, the Jewish People, as a Chosin People.

Obviously, chosenness is criminologically dangerous in becoming chosinness as are many theological concepts and transcendent constructs, in becoming most dangerous when they are religiously and secularly applied. What is often presented as the greatest religious good or secular virtue just as often presents itself as the greatest of criminal evils and vices.

The transcendent criminality of the theology of crime, in its many religious and secular variants, usually proceeds according to a particular theological construct - in one's being constructed by one God in acting for one's God, or in one constructing one's God in acting like a god in replacing one God for oneself - in a criminal concept of transcendent chosenness that generates a hateful religious or secular chosinness towards others.

Most studies of the Nazi-type criminality typically focus on sociological factors such as unemployment, political instability, and psychological processes such as projected inadequacy; and all of these are often quite evident among the rank and file of the poorly educated and skinhead type common criminal. However, the deeper and more intractable cause of the criminal rationality in the theology of crime is found in the very opposite kind of uncommon criminal, such as a highly educated and intelligent Jewish Dr. Baruch Goldstein, M.D., or German Dr. Josef Mengele M.D., Ph.D. Both Drs. Goldstein and Mengele appear, at first, to be exceptions to the criminal rule; but, actually, while they are exceptions in terms of criminal statistics, they constitute the criminal exception that proves the criminal rule of the theology of crime.

The criminal rule of the theology of crime can be a highly educational if not educated choice (in terms of a self-serving choice of one's education), but a true choice, nevertheless, of moral falsehood that's based on a moral lie of a criminally transcendent process, wherein the choice of one's chosen master race (as in the case of Mengele's secular theology) becomes the ultimate angel and devil of death against others. Chosenness becomes an avenging angel against everyone in the choice of religious or secular chosinness as a virtue for one's group and a vice for others.

In both religious and secular cases of the theology of crime, one's God, either one's transcendent self in one's religious God or in one's God-like group, replaces one God for all men in the misappropriation of God and disappropriation of men. Such chosen groups of people often pride themselves on being God like or even just like God, in their group; but I'm sure, God isn't like them, nor would God ever be proud of being referred to by any of them.

Quite obviously, there will never be a "never again" to the ever again of ethnic and religious cleansing that appears again and again, until the criminal rationality of the theology of criminally regarding one's group as chosen and others as chosin is exposed. Further, it must be countered at the same level at which it encounters others - the spiritual - in educating both young and old, the highly and poorly educated, in a true universal spiritual chosenness with which to combat self-serving, transcendent group chosinness.

Any educational step in a rehabilitation direction in reducing the recidivist rate of the theology of crime requires religious and secular cooperation. Past conflicts wherein this criminal problem was exploited or ignored in putting blame on too little or too much religion needs to be resolved. The resolution to the theology of crime requires a correct determination as to what is explicitly wrong in terms of being criminal in any transcendent theology that criminally manifests itself in any religious or secular group. In our secular society of religious freedom, we need to protect both secular and religious freedom by transcendent correcting of transcendent hate, without resorting to the hateful incorrectness of correctness.

Quite obviously, in the process of transcendent correction, a Jew, Moslem, or Christian, as a monotheistic example, will be less influenced by someone from another religion as much as by a source within one's own religion.

In this respect, I recall the example of Pope John XXIII, a truly holy man of God who was never holy at wholly others expense, who was regarded as holy by not only many Catholics, but, also, many Jews. He truly earned his Pontifical description of His Holiness when he stopped a Catholic religious service - certainly not as an anti-Catholic, but as a pro-Catholic - when a not so good, Good Friday reference to Jews evoked that age-old Christ-killer stereotype, and he removed it. He was aware how others saw this age-old reference in its group invidiousness, and no matter how much religious tradition was behind it and no matter how much it was revered by many religious, he corrected a transcendent hateful reference with a transcendent love of God.

A Jew could never have corrected it, nor could a Protestant, nor could nor should the State, but corrected it was, as it should have been.

We need more such transcendent correction for not only "holy" rituals but also holy books - in emphasizing the distinction between man's inspired words of hate in speaking about God in contrast to the inspiration of a loving God speaking to man.

Organizations such as the Freemasons, who have Protestants, Jews, Catholics and other religions in their spiritual fraternity, might take the educational lead in having their respective religious constituents create a hate index for their respective religions. The purpose of such a hate index would not be that of hateful conversion but, rather, Godly inversion - a la Pope John XXIII - of exposing, correcting and removing hate.

Other organizations, as well, both religious and secular, with ecumenical and universalist perspectives should consider combining their resources in a united front against the "chosin" theology of crime.

When the criminality is comparatively simple, such as in the case of the skinhead Matt, more vocational education and sensitivity training can be psychologically therapeutic. In the case of the violent abortion protestor such as Frank, more ecumenical education as to religious tolerance can be religiously therapeutic; in the case of the NOI, more inclusive programs can be socially therapeutic; and in dealing with cults, more total family support programs can do far more than the total of therapeutic deprogramming.

In other cases, however, as with the belief systems of the KKK, and the old and neo-Nazis - to include Judeo-Nazis - along with all those other new and old myriad of "chosin" theologies of religious and secular ethnocentrisms, only the transcendent therapy of transcendent correction from within can transcend the religious and secular criminality of the "chosin" theology of crime.

REFERENCES: Ryan, E. Scott. see "Born-Again" Masonry, The Philalethes, Vol. XLVII, April 1994, No. 2, 37-3, and "Born-Again" Masonry - II, The Philalethes, Vol. XLVII, June 1994, No. 3, 60-1; see also, The Masonic Conspiracy, The Philalethes, Vol. XLVI, Oct. 1993, No. 5, 104-105, and The Theology of Crime, The Philalethes, Vol. XLVII, Oct. 1994, No. 5, 112-113.

CHAPTER FIVE
Futuristic Universal Metaphysics

ABSTRACT

This paper points to a new way of thinking by examining the controversy as to the futuristic role of metaphysics being desireable or otherwise. The author presents a futuristic universal metaphysics in reference to the dynamics of evolving freedom, with the metaphor of driving a car into the future. He refers to a speech by Vaclav Havel, "On the Need for Transcendence in the Postmodern World", and to a critique of Havel in an article, "Is Transcendence Necessary?" by Edward Cornish , as president of the World Future Society. Dr. Ryan creates new wording in distinguishing Chosenness, in the universal spiritual choice of "The Fatherhood of God and Brotherhood of Man" from Chosinness, a sinful choice wherein Chosenness is religiously and secularly applied to the detriment of others. The author acknowledges the special influence of the Jesuits, Freemasons, and Buddhists, in formulating his futuristic, universal, metaphysical way of thinking.

The title of this article was engendered by Vaclav Haval's speech, "On the Need for Transcendence in the Postmodern World," in response to America's celebration of its independence and to the counter-response, "Is Transcendence Necessary," by Edward Cornish, as president of the World Future Society.

I would like to consider my own article as constituting a trilogy, of sorts, in agreeing with the major points of their different positions while continuing with their differing and my own different perspectives.

Haval presents his central argument for the need for self-transcendence in meeting post-modern needs for "unified meaning", in response to which Cornish states, "History shows us that metaphysical doctrines have only too often led to intense conflict rather than increased harmony".

Cornish proceeds to emphasize his point by referring to one particular historical involvement in Haval's capital city, Prague, among numerous savage religious battles, wherein outraged Protestants threw two Catholic councilors from the windows of Hradcany Castle, which later became the residence of Czech presidents. He then proceeds to question how any metaphysical propositions, even those as carefully non-doctrinal as those proposed by Havel, can escape the inevitable "fanaticism" of the metaphysical process.

Cornish's reminder, nevertheless, seems more relevant to others rather than to Haval, for Haval is well aware of the historical abuses of metaphysics in distancing himself from them. Haval is faulted a second time, however, not for his metaphysical reliance but for his metaphysical relevance... in relying upon the Anthropic Cosmological Principle and the Gaia Hypothesis. The Anthropic Principle suggests that the universe was expressly built for humans, and the Gaia Hypothesis portrays the world around us as a living Earth Mother, in response to which Cornish questions how unlikely it is that devout Christians, Moslems and other religionists will switch their allegiance to Gaia or Anthropic Cosmology.

My first reaction to their positions was to agree with Cornish as to the need for metaphysical caution, but to disagree with his pre-cautionary critique of Haval. It seemed as if Haval were put in a metaphysical bind, wherein he was faulted for relying on metaphysics on the supposition that metaphysics is inevitably fanatical and doctrinal, despite the fact that Haval goes to great lengths to disavow the traditional and the inevitable of not only fanatical doctrine but of any system of ideas contrary to "a science producing ideas that in a certain sense allow it to transcend its own limits".

It appeared to me that Haval was first pre-judged to be at fault in his metaphysical reliance based on a metaphysical judgment before all the metaphysical facts are in, that metaphysics, per se, is at fault. Secondly, Haval was thereupon post and past judged to be at fault as to the past in his metaphysical relevance, in not relying on the relevant metaphysics of religionists, which ironically was presented in Cornish's own example of the Hradcany Castle to be the central fault of relevant metaphysics.

Cornish is right to caution us about metaphysics, but those cautions are not right as to Havel's position, in the simultaneous cautions that Haval has not gone far enough in bringing too much of the past into the future, while going too far, in not being able to move into the future without moving with the relevant present.

It were as if Havel were being faulted for going back to the future and forward to the past... in not being able to get there from here... in not being able to get anywhere, metaphysically, from here. If he went metaphysically forward, he would inevitably bring the doctrinal fanaticism of the metaphysical past, and in any case, he couldn't possibly go to any metaphysical future without the metaphysical relevance of the past that is the present... that is the problem to begin with.

To employ the metaphor of a metaphysical scale, Havel's unlimited metaphysics were judged to be both too limiting and unlimited, in failing to weigh in within the limits of the metaphysical scale. The limits of the metaphysical scale, according to Cornish, are weighted against any metaphysical weighing, in the limits of Haval carrying too much and too little metaphysical baggage - in carrying too much of the metaphysical process of the past and too little of the metaphysical substance of the present.

In attempting to incorporate what's applicable in both of these positions - that of Haval's unlimiting metaphysical encountering with Cornish's counter of metaphysical limiting - the futuristic nexus revolves around one's choice of metaphysical choice in synthesizing the relevant with the futuristic and the particularistic with the universal. A futuristic metaphysics must not only transcend its own limits, as Haval suggests, but it must not transcend against others, as Cornish cautions.

If one wants to further categorize the metaphysical positions of Haval and Cornish, one can easily decipher a continental European philosophy of meta - of going beyond - physics versus that of a down home Yankee know-how: in preferring to know the scientific how rather than the philosophic how. Haval presents his adaptive philosophy of essence to which Cornish responds with his American logical positivism through a reliance on the tools of "a reformed social science".

At this stage of our journey, a further metaphor for our futuristic metaphysics is called for, in calling for a car with a manual transmission whose mission is transcendence - in accelerating in the right direction, a la Haval, while breaking at every wrong turn, a la Cornish.

In preparing to metaphysically drive in our futuristic car, Haval is cautioned by Cornish to check his metaphysical brakes for being too loose, in not being able to hold back the vehicular homicidal metaphysical momentum of the past; while Haval is also cautioned for being too hard on religionists, for having too much of an anti-lock braking mechanism in locking out what's religiously relevant.

The message appears to be more than that of safe metaphysical driving and more than that of drive at your own metaphysical risk, to don't risk driving at all, in being unsafe, metaphysically, at any speed... in under or over braking.

Cornish's recommendation of "reformed social science" in conjunction with the "possibilities of new electronic technologies" is correct as far as it goes, but it doesn't go far enough... metaphysically.

Nevertheless in analyzing the prospects for a futuristic metaphysics, I, for one, feel indebted to both Haval and Cornish - to Haval for putting his foot on the metaphysical accelerator, and to Cornish, for putting his on the brake.

In driving onward and, hopefully, upward on the road to a futuristic metaphysics, I'd recommend that we turn on the metaphysical ignition, as Haval does, while keeping our eyes on the speed limit, as Cornish advises. Before shifting into any futuristic gear, however, we need to put ourselves in the drivers' seat rather than in the passenger seat of our vehicular metaphysical choice.

The choice to be made is that of choosing how to unlimit our metaphysical freedom in facing metaphysical limits without being limited by them.

The greatest danger in unsafe metaphysical driving is not that of falling into historic potholes, although that remains a danger as Cornish correctly warns us; but the greatest danger is to assume - in making as ass of you and me - that freedom makes you free. One's freedom can be used to make oneself unfree, to include the modern process of one freedom to be unfree, in the post-modern processing of one's freedom.

Ironically, the process of American freedom as an increasingly one world modern process of free trade and economic liberalism appears to be far more post-modernly conservative in conserving by avoiding, in more avoidance of the implications of its freedom, than in the avoidance of freedom in the newly free escapes from freedom in the post-Communist world. As compared to the old world European philosophic essence that's both adopted and adapted by Haval, the one-world philosophy of American-styled freedom presents itself as far less than free in its daily constitutionals of freedom than it does in its Constitution of freedoms. Similarly, in a related avoidance of freedom, America has avoided the political consequences of the victory of its economic freedom over Marxist-Leninism, in avoiding the defeat of freedom in the world trade, trade-in of Market-Leninism.

Just as the avoidance of freedom can be as dangerous as its suppression, metaphysical choice cannot be avoided, as Cornish would like to avoid it, for no choice is a faulty choice of metaphysical default that produces the metaphysical faults of post-modern default that Haval wants to avoid.

In putting ourselves into metaphorical gear, metaphysically and futuristically, we need to be careful in keeping the road signs in sight, particularly the particularistic religious ones that Cornish refers to, while not being too careful in downshifting to a safer gear than necessary. While it's supposedly better to be safe than sorry, the pre-supposition to be metaphysically safe is to be futuristically sorry.

Correct metaphysical driving, however, is not metaphysical correctness, but, rather, correct metaphysical choice. Knowing what's immediately wrong or incorrect, nevertheless, doesn't mean that we know what's ultimately right. At our universal best, we need to know not what's singularly best, but what's best for our universal human nature and for our natural universe. Immediately, and at a minimum, we can begin to know what's most incorrect, at present, and most wrong for our future, in modifying what's most wrong into something that's least wrong and, hopefully, most right.

If we refuse to hope for metaphysical reform because the task is too hopelessly metaphysical, then we are left with the assumption of metaphysical inevitability - the metaphysics of ass over umption - in assuming all the faults of faulty and defaulted metaphysical choice as our only futuristic choice.

For those of us who drive stick shift automobiles, we're accustomed to the fifth gear as our highest gear, whereas Haval has shifted into a sixth futuristic gear of transcendence, for going even higher. Some might think that Haval is exceeding the metaphysical speed limit; and indeed he is, in exceeding the limits that we, as Americans, have imposed on ourselves.

There's an analogy, here, to the autobahn, one that many Americans who've been in the military have experienced, in driving on the speed limitless German autobahn. The analogy is that speed, even an unlimited one, need not be dangerous, provided that you're well trained and your car is engineered for that speed. At present, however, exceeding the speed limit can be dangerous in America, since almost anyone can get a driver's license and keep it into senility, and since most Americans cannot afford highly engineered Mercedes, Audis, and BMWs. Therefore, speeding is quite dangerous for Americans, but it need not be in a different context of better trained drivers and better engineered cars and roads.

A safety conscious American might say that Haval's acceleration is metaphysically breathtaking - to the degree of taking one's metaphysical breath away - as occurred in Cornish's out of breath metaphysical braking, in his metaphysical road sign of "Stop Before You Proceed".

My own road sign in driving towards futuristic metaphysics is to "Proceed With Caution, But Do Proceed", while being ready to brake, when necessary, in gearing into first in shifting upwards toward the futuristic gear. In further employing the metaphor of defensive metaphysical driving, it's imperative that we keep Cornish's road sign in mind, even when we're of a different mind, in watching out for the historical road conditions of danger - and in avoiding old and new metaphysical potholes.

One cannot, however, avoid the metaphysical dangers on the futuristic road by idling the engine and shifting into neutral metaphysics - in standing still in going nowhere... metaphysically. Just as the best defense is offense, the best metaphysics is to go beyond taking historical offense to taking the offense, futuristically, without giving offense... in falling into the historical, modern or post-modern offensiveness of metaphysical fault or default.

We need to be watchful, so as to see what to avoid ahead, rather than to avoid seeing what's ahead. If we drive correctly, if our car is well engineered, and if our vehicular metaphysical acceleration is monitored by the right quality control, then we should be able to drive around rather than through old and new metaphysical hazards.

However, in driving ahead we need to check our rear view mirror in shifting into first, not only to avoid any rear end collision in colliding with the reckless driving of past metaphysics, but, also, to harness the religionist momentum of the past and present. In so doing, we can see the Abrahamic tradition that gave birth to the monotheistic religions of Judaism, Christianity, and Islam. Nevertheless, we also need to incorporate other spiritual traditions and the insights in the Way of the Buddha, in particular.

We need to observe, as some of my Buddhist friends have observed, how much violence is associated with the history of monotheism to include the violence of Abraham, himself, in his willingness to obey God to the homicidal extent of killing his son as a sacrifice. Sacrifice seems to permeate the Abrahamic tradition from the religious sacrifice of the Jews, to Jesus as the Sacrificial Lamb of the Christians, to the sacrifice of oneself and others in the Islamic Surrender to the Will of Allah.

In reference to the futuristic metaphysical goal of universal human brotherhood, we can observe that the great monotheistic religions of Judaism, Christianity and Islam, as great as they are in their belief, have often been less than great in their practice of that belief. All three have at one time or another persecuted not only each other, but themselves, in intra-religious holy wars even more unholy in their ungodliness than the inhumanity of inter-religious crusades, pogroms, jihads, inquisitions (those of the English as well as the Spanish to include Protestants along with Catholics), and "God gave your land to me" religious and ethnic cleansings.

One can easily understand why many would like to keep God out of our metaphysical future in their belief that more of God has brought less to man and, therefore, less of God should bring more to man. It's easy to understand this secular belief in religious non-belief without agreeing with it, for there exists a fatal flaw in the secular humanistic critique of God and Man. This flaw lies neither in humanism nor in God, but in man's proclivity of secular belief in man as God, when he rejects the religious belief in a God for all men. The well-intended secular humanistic intention that less of God brings more to man is correct, but in a quite different way than intended. That more was alluded to by Dostoevski in The Brothers Karamazov in the statement, "If there is no God, then anything is possible," to include more of any secular evil in compounding religious evil.

Nevertheless, this suspicion of the very idea of God in any man's religion is historically well founded in the illustration that Cornish presents among countless others; and it is one that needs to be understood in its futuristic implications. One can understand, however, without rejecting the idea of an understanding God that some men rejected in the practice of religion, even more than in the secular denial of it.

Let us metaphysically allow for a futuristic understanding of God; but let us proceed into second gear with a more universal understanding to incorporate the traditions of the Great Spirit of indigenous peoples and the Ultimate One of Buddhism as a supplement rather than a substitute for the Judeo-Christian and Abrahamic traditions.

One can assert that metaphysical oneness can be a source of both good and evil, in bringing people together in love or in pulling them apart in hate. My own religious hypothesis is that the more narrow and straight one's religiosity in reference to one God, the greater one's propensity to go to wide and crooked extremes in denigrating others.

Accordingly, while the lesser gods of Buddhism and the greater saints of Catholicism, as the two major religions of East and West, share some similarities in offending some fundamentalists, they also share a futuristic propensity for metaphysically countering the traditions of ethnocentricity, traditionalism, literalism and fanaticism in some other religions. Some of these other religious traditions fuel a past and present metaphysics of Divine Hate, in a Theology of Crime in offending against others, in the morally dirty crimes of ethnic and religious cleansings.

In accelerating in second gear, we encounter chosenness, the Chosen People tradition of the Hebrew Covenant that also manifests itself in the Christian Covenant. Both of these covenants of chosenness culminate in the Judeo-Christian Bible of the Old and New Testaments. Some purists may assert that Judeo-Christian is a misnomer because of major differences between Judaism and Christianity; but regardless of those obvious differences, the major similarity of chosenness justifies the Judeo-Christian hyphenate, in my opinion.

In reference to Jewish, Christian and Moslem religionists, Cornish is quite correct in cautioning Havel that these People of the Book - be it Old Testament, New Testament or The Koran - are unlikely to choose to turn in their old books in order to turn to new choices inherent in the Gaia Hypothesis and the Anthropic Cosmological Principle.

Chosenness, defined as universal spiritual chosenness, in choosing one God for all men, is integral to any humanistic interactive relationship with God. In futuristic theology, one might describe it as being "on-line with God".

Nevertheless, there's an inherent religious danger in the spiritual metaphysics of chosenness, in plugging in one's religion to keep oneself On-Line, in keeping others plugged out... in their being religiously Off-Line, downed and out of the system. The uplifting metaphysical software of an interactive program of universal spiritual chosenness - in everyone's choice of choosing and being chosen - can degenerate into a programmed choice in the self-serving religious hardware of being hard on others in wearing them down... while one is easy on one's self in lifting oneself up in a group holiness that's wholly at others expense.

The holistic negation of the one and the same holiness of one God for everyone occurs when one God becomes one's God only, in a God gave this or that to me in my taking it from you. In both historical and recent examples, the taking of others land not to mention, "slaying of the inhabitants thereof," by some Christian missionaries and some Jewish settlers has given the "chosen" Judeo-Christian tradition a less than Godly heritage that no truly Godly Christian or Jew can be proud of. The colonial exploitation of "The White Man's Burden" was aided and abetted by "the false chosenness of the Godly Burden", in making God an unholy burden by burdening others (and God) with one's own chosenness.

Therefore, while chosenness in its universal spiritual dimension can be a metaphysical blessing, its application, be it religious or secular, can be a metaphysical curse. The best protection from the proclivity of the blessed choice of chosenness to become a cursed sinful choice - what I term chosinness in the choice of sin in sinning against non-chosen others - is spiritual universalism.

The traditions of spiritual universalism in the East and West must be brought together and used as a rigorous monitor, in monitoring the religious tendency to turn universal spiritual chosenness into self-serving religious chosinness. Only when chosenness is metaphysically defined as God being chosen by and for all men, will there ever be a futuristic theology that can function as a metaphysical counter to the "ever again" of religious and ethnic cleansing - in a "never again" to any group being chosin (in the sinful choice of being perceived by others as less chosen than themselves).

In shifting upward from the first gear of one's God as one God for everyone and the second gear of universal spiritual chosenness, we find ourselves developing more secular speed but less spiritual power in the third gear of the secular humanistic acceleration of the Enlightenment.

Once again, we find ourselves with strengths and weaknesses and virtues and vices in needing to know when to accelerate and when to brake, in the acceleration of secular humanism. One of the metaphysical potholes of secular humanism, and one that I referred to earlier, is a fatal flaw in its critique of God and Man. That flaw lies in the belief in man as God when a religious belief in God is rejected.

The Enlightenment philosophy in the West was quite different from Buddhist Enlightenment in the East. In freeing Western man from a transcendent God, it left him with a transcendent belief without a belief in the Transcendent, a transcendence without the Transcendent; in a belief in any belief - culminating in laissez-faire (lousey-faire) capitalism, international socialism (Communism) national socialism (Nazism), and more recently, national communism (in the newly free escape from freedom in many former communist lands).

Nazism, in particular, was a logical development rather than an aberration in the land of Goethe, of a secular humanistic enlightenment that defined what was good for oneself and one's group without reference to any universal God as the basis of morality. That humanism - in all its human perfection - could become perfectly inhumane was a paradox, but not a contradiction. Such a development is quite logical when man transcends himself without the Transcendent. The fact that the religious history of man acting in the name of his one God was often quite ungodly, only became even more godless when man secularly transcended himself by putting himself in God's place.

Both the religious ungodliness and secular godlessness of man proceeded neither from God nor from man alone, but from disassociation of the correct association of God and man.

Therefore, a correct metaphysical conceptualization of the Divine is more than a matter of personal faith in the intellectual assent of one's will to one's religion. The correct metaphysical association between God and men involves the collective will to perfect one's religious faith in being perfected in one God for all men, rather than being perfect in one's faith for oneself or one's group.

The disassociation of God and Man in either believing in one God for oneself instead of for all men as brothers, or in denying God by acting like a god, with the secular dogmas of human predestination according to evolution, class, economics, ethnicity, or more recently, the cognitive elite (whose cognition as to others shows itself to be less than elite), explains the greatest metaphysical irony of all: good and evil become one and the same with the greatest good justifying the greatest evil. Whether it be religious or secular totalitarianism, what is totally good becomes totally bad, with the best virtue justifying the worst vice. The ultimate vice of this religious or secular virtue proceeds from the incorrect association of oneness with God by defining one's own God or good in terms of what is good for oneself in one's group.

The Hitlerian refrain of "Ein Volk, Ein Reich, Ein Fuehrer" (One People, One Realm, One Leader) is the ultimate secular version of ethnic cleansing that proceeded from the secular version of chosenness: a religious cleansing wherein the religious concept of a Chosen People became that of a "Chosin" People - a People of Sin - when a new Chosen People, the Master Race, appropriated chosenness to themselves in eliminating Jews and others as "chosin".

Whether man denies himself in the name of God or denies God in the name of man, men have disassociated themselves from God in the death of Man rather than God. Mankind's unkind history of religiously and secularly appropriating oneness with the one true God to himself, alone, at the expense of nature (which calls forth the GAIA Hypothesis), or to his group, to the exclusion of others, at the expense of others human nature (which calls forth the Anthropic Principle), has been a persistent metaphysical lie in opposition to the everlasting truth of a universal inclusive God.

There is a need for a futuristic metaphysical conspiracy to conspire for God in a human brotherhood and sisterhood of those who believe in one God for everyone over one's God for oneself or one's group. Religion needs not only to be acknowledged, as Cornish acknowledges it, but respected, as well, if there is to be any progress in getting well on to a futuristic metaphysics from the here and now of religion. However, the respect due religion is a spiritual respect, in respecting religion as God meant it to be rather than as man has made it to be.

The metaphysical obscurity of God is so dense, however, that some have already said that God is dead; and others might say that if God's alive, he's a well kept secret. The sublime secret of futuristic metaphysics must be that God need not be a dead secret, although God has been kept secret by those who do evil in the name of good by putting their belief in their God, or in their secular substitute for God for themselves, in the place of one God for everyone.

The futuristic metaphysical conspiracy should be a quirk of faith in being unique in being universal, in being existentially free in being essentially bound in the spiritual foundations of a universal God. The conspiracy is to be the same and to be different, in having the same faith as others in their religious faith in God without rejecting others according to religion. The conspiratorial metaphysics lies in this religious quirk of faith that goes beyond religion without rejecting religion, in attempting to build what has yet to be built and house what has yet to be housed in the spiritual metaphysical architecture of a religious Fatherhood of God in addition to the Fatherhood in religion, and in building a Brotherhood in one God to supplement any one Brotherhood in religion.

In so proceeding, in building upon the Abrahamic religious foundations and upon the secular humanistic foundations of The Enlightenment, we also need to incorporate and build upon The Way of Enlightenment of the Buddha. The Enlightenment philosophy of the West needs to be integrated with the philosophic Way of Enlightenment of the Buddha - in a yin and yang balancing of one's transcendent self with the transcendent denial of self.

The next metaphysical gear, that of the fourth gear of ecumenical universalism has to be more broadly ecumenical in order to keep up with the increased breadth and depth of futuristic metaphysics. The Ecumenical Movement has made enormous progress since Vatican II and the most holy Pope John XXIII (who was never holy at wholly others expense), in improving Catholic - Protestant - Anglican - Orthodox relations, and in denouncing the historic scandal of anti-Semitism. There has also been some progress on the Catholic-Muslim level, although much more needs to be done in removing limits to mutual tolerance rather than in joint moves to put limits on birth control. Nevertheless, the ecumenism of a futuristic metaphysics is not a prayer that "They may all be one", but, rather, a prayer that any one religious minority may be tolerated by any one and all majority. Further, much more sensitivity is needed in reference to non - Abrahamic spiritualities - as evidenced in Pope John Paul's Sri Lankan visit where his unfortunate description of Buddhism as negative was most negatively received.

Such negative descriptions are most ecumenically negative, indeed, in attesting to a negative disregard in the ill-chosen statement of a well-intentioned Pope. Although my own statements don't carry the weight of the Papacy, I like to think that they carry the weight of truth, in stating from my Jesuit educated Catholic background that the way of the Buddha has been the most positive experience of my life.

In the future, and I'd recommend the near future, we need to hear more from our Buddhist brothers, who know us; and we need to hear less from some of us, be it from a Pope mobile or a televangelist in Mobile, Alabama, about what they think about others whose wisdom they don't know.

In reference to ecumenical universalism, I recall what I consider to be the best definition from a conversation a number of years ago with a Vietnamese Buddhist monk. At that time, in having been theologically educated with the analytic rigor of the Jesuits, I was foolhardy enough to assume that I could apply Western theological analytic criteria in my inquiry into Eastern spirituality. After attempting to theologically define, categorize and delineate, the gentle and patient monk replied as follows:

"When you get to the top of the mountain, what is more important... how you get there or that you're there?" To which I replied by nodding the obvious.

"Also, when you look down from the highest point, doesn't everything below tend to look the same?" In response to which I replied again by nodding.

To this day, I know of no better description of ecumenical universalism than the silent answers inherent in his non-adversarial rhetorical questions that answered themselves. As a final comment on Christian - Buddhist relations which I believe can and should be improved, I know of many Catholic religious who have worked with Buddhist monks, not one of whom, to my personal knowledge, had ever referred to Buddhism with expressions other than those characterizing it as most peaceful and beautiful.

The next gear is that of the fifth gear of metaphysical freedom, the cruising gear of choosing freedom not only for oneself but for others. Freedom of any kind, however, is easier said than done, as America's Constitution of freedom, for example, cannot unsay all that's said and not done about the failures of freedom in the daily constitutionals of America's problems with its freedom.

Martin Luther, who took offense at the Catholic freedom of indulgences, indulged in his own Protestant freedom to give offense during the German Peasants revolt by refusing to protest against the German landlords, in allowing them to take more freedom for themselves in disallowing more freedom for their subjects. The unfree peasants, who quoted the freedom verses of Luther's Bible of freedom, took their faith in freedom seriously in a bloody revolt for their freedom. They put their faith for salvation in Luther's faith for salvation by faith alone, to find themselves faithlessly alone, in being bloodied not only by their landlords, but by Luther, who kept his faith with the landlords rather than with the Lord.

As a result, they experienced the lost of their very physical salvation, along with their faith in salvation by their freedom, alone, in the experience of their Protestant patron of freedom patronizing the freedom of the Protestant establishment to the total disestablishment of their freedom and themselves.

I refer to this phenomenon as the Lutheran Dilemma, which is a dilemma of freedom by no means limited to Luther...in one's taking freedom for oneself in taking it away from others.

The next stage in the accelerating struggle for freedom was neither a Catholic nor a Protestant struggle, but, rather, a Masonic one in the American Revolution: one that is commemorated in millions of exchanges every day in the Masonic symbol of the all seeing eye on America's dollar. While the almighty dollar may have lost some or even all of its might, to the yen and deutschmark, the one all-seeing eye of its freedom has made its world wide mark in others yen for the modern process - if not substance of its freedom.

Not only was George Washington, as the Father of his Country and the military leader of the American War for freedom, a Mason, but many other founding fathers who wrote the Constitution of the United States were Masons as well. What they shared in common was a strong influence and adherence to Masonic principles as to freedom from religious and political dogmatism. There is considerable but largely unknown historical documentation that shows a direct linkage between the Masonic Constitutions of the Reverend Anderson, a Scottish Presbyterian minister, (often referred to as the Anderson or Masonic Constitutions) and the American Constitution, which closely follows its tenets and principles.

Some anti-Masons, who contrary to common assumptions are more numerous in Protestant than Catholic circles, may dispute this association as no more than a coincidence; but it cannot be disputed that if it is a coincidence - it is a most extraordinary coincidence, indeed. Such an unlikely coincidence, in fact, would probably exceed a scientific probability correlation association in excess of .01 - which in common parlance translates to a random probability that's not only most improbable, but's as next to impossible as one can possibly measure the probability of any possibility.

Despite the advance of freedom in the American metaphysics of its revolution, however, the constitutional system of American freedom presided over a revolting system of slavery that quoted its own nativist Bible of freedom to itself in lighting burning crosses as it ignited the burning fires of an American holocaust against Native Americans.

Only now, as we begin the twenty-first century, over two centuries after America's war against England and over one century since its Civil War against itself, is America ready to redefine its own history from that of "How the West was Won" to "How the West was Lost". The manifest destiny of its westward expansion was, manifestly, an expanded Final Solution for the destiny of the Native Americans. As a statistical fact, it destined for elimination a higher percentage of the Native American population (to exceed 90%), than even that of the deadly efficient Nazi Final Solution (in finalizing approximately 66%) as to the chosen people...in that recurrent chosen - chosin metaphysical process in the Nazi's choosing themselves as a Master Race.

America, however, did move ahead in constitutionalizing its virtue of freedom, despite its vices in denying freedom to some of its own as well as to some others. Further, that freedom continues to work, sometimes well in freely owning up to the needs of others, and sometimes not as well in its freedom to disown the needs of others, in continuing to work in spite of the abuse of freedom without which freedom cannot be free. One might characterize that abuse as those on the left doing more than what's needed and those on the right doing less than what's needed.

While there are new threats to that freedom in correctness - be it political, sexual, racial or whatever, in whatever is legislatively correct, in the hate legislation that hates hate in the hateful legislative correctness of correcting hate by legislating correct thoughts - America continues, as the modern process of freedom, to move towards a post-modern metaphysics of freedom. Its special strengths reside in its all-seeing eye in seeing the freedoms of speech and religion, in continuing to see an all-encompassing civil libertarianism, wherein no one opinion or religion is more free or correct than another in being corrected or in being guaranteed more freedom than another.

The next and last gear for now, in moving at present with the momentum of the past, in shifting into our futuristic sixth gear, is that of self-transcendence, even though transcendence, itself, is in question (a la Havel and Cornish). Although the metaphysical options have increased, (per example Havel's Gaia Hypothesis and Anthropic Principle), to include new and old options from East and West, the most conservative options (per example the religionists referred to by Cornish) appear to be predominant.

Rather than the freedom and danger of a metaphysical Prometheus unbound, who steals fire from the Gods, more people prefer to steal themselves away, in being religiously bound, in lighting ungodly fires in the name of God in setting fire to religious liberality. A Protestant Professor of Theology at Princeton University was quoted as stating that the religious future seemed to belong to a reformed Catholicism and to a mature Pentecostalism, with the more liberal main-line Protestant denominations continuing to fade away. In a related observation, one can also refer to a growing fundamentalism among Muslims and Jews.

Perhaps this trend is a little more than an awareness of the insecurity of transcending old transcendence in new metaphysical opportunities. Perhaps, also, as is evident in the dangerous metaphysical process of chosenness - chosinness, there may be a fear of a recurrence of any new choice of transcendence, with or without the Transcendent, in retreating to the old and secure process of one's already chosen transcendence within a fundamentalistically known religiousity or secularity.

Nevertheless, regardless of the psychology of metaphysics, fear of transcendence will not remove the fact of transcendence - be it with or without fault or by default - in the reality of futuristic metaphysics.

Proceeding, even with a conservative "Fear of the Lord is the beginning of all wisdom," is preferable to a liberal dispensation not to proceed at all in ignoring the relevance of metaphysical realities.

We should be fearful, in "fearing only fear itself," in metaphysically fearing the fear of metaphysics. The greatest fear that we should have is not a metaphysical one, but a futuristic one, in the fear of our futuristic metaphysics being defined for us by the past or in not being defined at all.

The result of allowing others to define it for us is evidenced in the continuing history of past and present religious and secular dogmatism. Freedom, itself, in freedom processing itself, can become dogmatic, in itself. Unless freedom evolves continually, in learning from the past, and futuristically, in learning for the future, freedom will devolve. In the postmodern devolution of the modern evolution of freedom, the substance of evolving freedom devolves in any one process of freedom that denies the substance of freedom in processing others or in one's processing of oneself.

Freedom has to be metaphysically and futuristically defined or else it defines its faults as its self, in a process of free default. That process of default produces faulty processing, wherein an undefined and unlimited process of freedom defines and limits the substance of freedom into a faulty freedom. In the processing of the free-prefixed process in the postmodern posting of one freedom as an unfree process, there is the one freedom to be unfreely one and the same. That one freedom is in conforming to the free prefix norm of free-trade, free-market, free-society or free-whatever, with the greatest freedom for the free-prefixed process.

In the unfree processing of the free-prefixed process, there is an unfree expectation of conformity to the means and ends of that process, in the processed means of taking one way to freedom, in taking the end substance of one's freedom away. Ironically, in the prefixing of freedom, one is expected to be unfree in one's freely conforming to any one free-prefixed process...in internalizing one impersonal process as one's personal substance.

Postmodern freedom, therefore, personally particularizes an impersonal universal process in personal conformity to impersonal process. The particularistic personalisms of one's particular free person become particularly free of one's personal substance of freedom in one universal freedom of process...in one's freedom to be unfree in one freedom.

In the postmodern posting process of freedom, one's freedom is processed to the extent that free process not only replaces the substance of freedom but substitutes itself as the substance of one's freely processed self. One is most free to be most commonly free in any one free process with others...in the unfree process of the self-processing of one's uncommonly free self.

Without freedom, transcendence cannot transcend one's self, but even with freedom, transcendence for oneself doesn't free one of one's self...in the freedom of self-transcendence.

In the future, with or without a religious God, spiritual chosenness, scientific secular humanism, ecumenical universalism or the transcendent metaphysics of evolving freedom, the metaphysical freedom of a futuristic universal metaphysics will be free in defining itself - for good or for evil.

That freedom, however, as well intentioned as it might be, in shifting forward with the skill and caution of careful acceleration and braking in each progressive gear, has a manifest destiny of its own in the Lutheran Dilemma that is everyone's metaphysical dilemma with freedom. That dilemma rests in defining how to metaphysically ascend in taking any one freedom to transcend, without transcending by descending in taking freedom - one's own or others - away.

CHAPTER SIX

Case Studies of the Psychological and Forensic Assessment of Parental Child Abuse

ABSTRACT:

Dr. Ryan presents a forensic analytic critique of the Court process of applying psychological assessment to criminal cases. He presents five cases from the New Jersey Court files of a court appointed clinical psychologist to demonstrate how psychological assessment, even in the traditional therapeutic area of parental child abuse, is inadequate. Dr. Ryan recommends that forensic analysis rather than psychological analysis should be applied in all criminal cases. In special cases where therapeutic psychological intervention is necessary, forensic assessment would remain as a necessary supplement to psychological assessment. In the majority of criminal cases, however, Dr. Ryan recommends that forensic assessment, diagnosis, classification and treatment should go beyond being a supplement to being a substitute for psychological intervention in the justice system.

The following five cases were taken from the case files of a court appointed clinical psychologist whose career specialty is the psychological assessment of parents, wherein the custody of their abused or neglected children is to be determined. These cases represent a form of criminality that is usually relegated to the realm of psychological analysis rather than forensic analysis. Although some of these cases do belong in the realm of traditional psychological therapeutic assessment, some do not. A significant number of these kind of abuse cases belong more to forensic analysis than psychological analysis; and an even greater number call for a new combination of forensic and psychological analysis.

The application of a newly combined specific forensic and psychological analysis for assessing and treating criminality is not to be equated with forensic psychology, in general, which often blurs crucial analytic distinctions. It is the intent of these case studies to clarify the analytic differences between psychological and forensic assessment in cases such as these by applying a forensic assessment of not only the client-offender, but of the court mandated psychological assessment. This forensic assessment can range from a necessary supplement to a necessary substitute for psycho-logical assessment. In either case, however, it is necessary for all criminal cases; whereas psychological assessment is necessary in only a minority of criminal cases.

The cases presented here are far more illustrative than common criminal non-abuse cases in applying the nexus of psychological and forensic assessment. Criminological research studies have consistently demonstrated that psychological assessment, diagnoses, classification and treatment are mostly irrelevant to most criminality. (1) In my previous study, Therapeutic Justice and Child Abuse, I presented case studies of the abuses of the therapeutic, psychological medical model by use of verbatim references to the psychological assessments, diagnoses, classifications and treatment recommendations in the open and closed court files of serious child abuse cases to include murder. (2) All of the cases in my Therapeutic Justice study were from the Commonwealth of Pennsylvania, whereas all of the cases in this study are from the State of New Jersey. In both states and in both studies, confidential court files were used; and it was only by virtue of my professional criminological association with Court appointed professionals in forensics and clinical psychology that I was able to access these cases.

On both a professional and personal level there's an urgent need for more confidential Court files to be accessed by more forensic researchers. As evidenced in both my Therapeutic Justice study and in this study, operational forensics research needs to be systemically expanded in criminal justice. Furthermore, it can be evidenced by my own studies and others that forensic research into confidential Court case files can be conducted with-out any violation of personal privacy or confidentiality requirements in the justice system.

The unfortunate miscarriage of child protection and the tragic results of the misapplication of therapy in the justice system that I reported upon in my study of Therapeutic Justice and Child Abuse are not repeated, fortunately, in the results of the cases in this study. The more fortunate determinations in the cases before us were determined in no small measure by the psychologist involved assigning first priority to the protection of the children involved. Although the psychological assessment in the following cases reflects the non-forensic analysis we'd expect from a psychologist, salient forensic factors are not ignored as they often are in other cases, as documented in Therapeutic Justice and Child Abuse. (2)

Therefore, as a result of the dynamics of the cases, themselves, and the highly responsible dynamic of the psychologist, himself, we can better analyze the dynamics of both psychological and forensic assessments. These case studies also allow us to not only distinguish forensic assessment from psychological assessment, but, also, to point out that they need to work in conjunction with each other rather than in competition with each other. The precise dynamics of the how to and the where of working together needs much more work, but these case studies point the way to working that out. (3) The cases in this study are presented in the same manner that those in the study of Therapeutic Justice and Child Abuse was presented in accessing the psychological assessments, verbatim, from the Court case files. In the process, the real names of the clients, as the psychologist refers to them, or the offenders, as the forensic analysis would refer to them, were deleted and changed.

CASE 1: SARAH

PSYCHOLOGICAL EVALUATION
NAME: Sarah, Age 41

REASONS FOR EVALUATION:
The evaluation was conducted pursuant to a court order to assess the Client's psychological capacity to assume care of her two-year-old son who has been in foster care since he was six months old. The Division is seeking to terminate the birth mother's parental rights in order to free D for adoption.

BASIS OF EVALUATION:
Rorschach Psychodiagnostic   Structured and open-ended interviews
Complaint for guardianship by DAG
Reviewed By Not Relied Upon:
Drug and Alcohol Evaluation by CADC, 6-23-99
Drug and Alcohol Evaluation by CADC, 7-6-94
Drug and Alcohol Evaluation by CAC, 8-12-94
Psychological Evaluation of Sarah by Ed.D. 6-24-94

BACKGROUND INFORMATION:
According to Sarah she "...grew up in an Italian family and had lots of love". But questioning elicited details that were more unpleasant than the image evoked by her general statement. Her parents remained together till Sarah was about three and her father moved out because "...my mother drank a lot and was always out". Sarah and her mother stayed together, but she spent a lot of time at the home of her paternal grandparents "...because I wanted to be with him". When she was about five, her mother asked her if she wanted to go on a shopping trip, but she declined in favor of visiting with her father's family. The mother left with her three-year-old sister, "R" and did not return, "When we got home, everything was gone except my stuff." She never saw her mother again till she was in

her early teens and there was a brief visit after it became known that the mother had cancer. However, "she called once when I was six or seven, on my birthday to say 'Hello'".

Sarah went to live in the home of her paternal grandparents and was cared for by an aunt who was in her mother's age range. She is unsure if her father lived in the house, although she recalls that he was there to kiss her goodnight. He had a relationship with another woman, whom he married when Sarah was 12. Sarah joined them in their new home and was treated "just like I was her daughter". Her father made a good living as a butcher and later had his own shop and grocery store at the Jersey Shore. According to Sarah she, "never wanted for anything" and had horseback riding lessons. Her father and stepmother had two sons who are now in their mid-twenties. They are still together. He has heart problems and is semi-retired.

Her mother married "L" who had lived upstairs from them when Sarah was a preschooler. He played in a band and drank alcohol. The couple had four children and "always did without". She recalls that her sister R had few material possessions and was "into my stuff" when they visited once when R was about 11. Sarah's mother succumbed to the cancer about 14 years ago. She had remained out of her daughter's life virtually all of the time since she left.

Sarah "struggled a little bit," but did earn a high school diploma in the regular education program. After high school she because a certified nurse. She does not pass out medication, but cares for infirm people. Her longest period of employment was two years in a convalescent center during the second half of the 80s. She also has done private duty care for paraplegics. She was most recently employed in 1992.

Sarah became pregnant at 15 and married "J" who was about five years older. She bore a son by the same name and the marriage lasted eight years. She left with their son because her husband was a substance abuser who sought immediate gratification and would not plan for the future. She and seven-year-old J moved in with three men and she began a relationship with "L" whom she later married. During this period she worked as a bartender. (She had moved with her father and stepmother from Essex County to Long Beach Island and Toms River areas when she was about 13 and started his own business.) Apparently L was much more responsible than her first husband: he had a good paying job with the public works department of the local municipality. Their union produced "H" and "A" his daughter from another marriage came to live with them. He separated from Sarah in 1992 because of her involvement with heroin. He retained custody of H and they were later divorced. J, her son by the first marriage, "didn't like Harvey Cedars" and had gone back to live with his father and paternal grandmother.

Sarah first tried marijuana when she was 18, but does not consider it to have presented problems for her. She did not drink alcohol till her early 20s and says its consumption has not caused problems either. She has suffered a series of four auto accidents between 1987 and 1994 which left her seriously injured and in considerable pain. In each accident she was a passenger and each involved a different driver. She was prescribed a variety of painkillers and antidepressants. She believes that her drug dependence developed during this period. Apparently her first husband was a state police informant (Sarah demurs to call him such) and obtained heroin for her in the late 1980s. She has used heroin inconsistently over the last six years. She "successfully" completed a rehabilitation program in 1993, but, nevertheless, began using again. She claims to have been drug free for the last nine months.

Sarah acknowledges a history of depressive episodes beginning in her late 20s "right after I had H". She has been treated four times in the last ten years and two episodes (1991 and 1993) required hospitalization. She does not link them to external events, "I had everything I needed. I just didn't like something about me". During the depressive periods she felt that "there was no hope" and would sleep long hours. But there were periods of agitation as well, "L used to say 'Are you all right? Do you know it's three o'clock in the morning?'" She considered these hours to be her private time. During the day she had to take care of newborn H. Sarah recalls, "I didn't crash (during the day). I always had a lot of energy during those years". She could not provide specifics as to the frequency and duration of these episodes. Typically she would consult a physician who would prescribe antidepressants – amitriptyline is one she remembers – and she would take the medication for "a little while" (two to four weeks) or "a few months" as needed. Eventually she would wean herself from the medication and find that she was no longer depressed without it.

Sarah was arrested in 1993 for possession with intent to sell near a school zone. She retained her freedom as part of a plea bargain. She began serving a minimum of 18 months of a four-year sentence in September of 1995 for violation of probation after she was arrested for shoplifting in May of 1994. She admitted to "some speeding tickets earlier" and to having her license suspended in 1992 for driving while intoxicated after she drank two glasses of homemade wine at a party and "the (breathalyzer) needle just went over the line". She acknowledges "some other municipal charges" for shoplifting that are "being cleared up" by her attorney and says her present incarceration is her only one.

Presently Sarah is on "full minimum" and has a record of good behavior since being incarcerated. She receives daily counseling through the Ackerman program on grounds. Her earliest release date is December of 1996. She has applied for residence in a halfway house and believes that she will serve out her sentence there after she completes phase one of the Ackerman program in another two months. Once in the halfway house she believes she will be able to work and "go home" on weekends.

OBSERVATIONS AND IMPRESSIONS:

Sarah was evaluated in a classroom of the Edna Mahn Correction Facility by prior arrangement. She is of average height (5'-1") and overweight (155 lbs.). She was dressed in jeans, a sweatshirt and athletic shoes. Her hair is shoulder length. She wore small button earrings. Makeup was not apparent. There is a small scar under her right eye which resulted from one of her accidents and she volunteered that "...my whole face is wired together". She is totally blind in her right eye. She wore glasses during the part of the evaluation that required vision.

There was nothing remarkable about her posture, stance or gait on brief examination. She displayed no unusual mannerisms or speech patterns. Her eye contact was adequate and she related in a relaxed and friendly manner. Her intelligence is certainly normal and probably above average. She was alert, adequately oriented in the three spheres and fully comprehending of the situation. Her memory for both recent and remote events was serviceable, but selective. Her associative processes were fluid, but were not loose, tangential or bizarre. There was not evidence of delusions, hallucinations or any disorder in the form of her thinking. There was no evidence or primary process thinking into consciousness.

Sarah considers her health "good" in spite of occasional back pain stemming from the auto accident in July of 1993. She is not taking any prescription or over-the-counter medications. She has no problem eating or sleeping. She admits to neither obsessive thoughts nor compulsive actions and denies ideas of reference. She admits to thoughts of "going to sleep and not waking up again" after she lost a severely premature baby prior to 1981. She had similar feelings after her most recent car accident when she feared that should would not be able to walk again. She denies any thoughts of homicide.

Sarah's mood was appropriately sober for the circumstances. The range and intensity of her affect was somewhat constricted and occasionally inappropriate as when she smiled while discussing painful aspects of her life. Her self-control was generally adequate although she did become tearful and needed a few moments to compose herself toward the end of the evaluation. Either consciously or unconsciously Sarah obstructed communication by minimizing her own role in her present difficulties (e.g., Everybody smoked a joint.") and diverting attention onto others (e.g., "My husband used drugs. He got me to use them."). The nature and scope of the procedures as well as the limits of confidentiality were reviewed with Sarah and she agreed to cooperate. The impression was that she was capable of producing valid and reliable findings.

PSYCHOMETRIC FINDINGS:

The number of responses that Sarah made to the Rorschach test is low, but still within normal limits and allows for comparison of her protocol with the normative data. Two features of the record are immediately obvious: the Coping Deficit Index is elevated and she has not developed a preferred style for approaching problems. The analysis of her psychological organization and functioning shall proceed from these findings. By their mid-teens most individuals have developed a preferred style (not necessarily a capacity) for approaching problems and managing the stresses of life. They tend to be either objective and dispassionate or emotional and interactive. One style is not necessarily superior to the other, but ambitents, such as Sarah, are at a clear disadvantage because they tend to oscillate between the two extremes and are inefficient in managing their lives. In order not to bias the interpretation her protocol was compared to the norms for people with the same type of disability. Even with this allowance her Coping Deficit Index is more elevated than 94% of the reference group. Therefore, the finding that she is in better-than-average equilibrium and has resources to spare is immediately suspicious. Closer analysis shows that her internal resources are barely within normal limits and it is her unrealistically low stress level that creates the spurious surplus (no one in the reference groups is as unstressed as she). How she maintains her equilibrium and the price she pays to do so are discussed below in the paragraph dealing with her cognitive processing. Sarah is about as prone as the average ambient to be drawn into emotionally charged situations. Her affective life appears somewhat more bland than the average adult's. However, there is indication that when her emotions are aroused they will be discharged in an amplified and poorly modulated manner. The index of depression is marginal even now when she claims not to be depressed.

Sarah's degree of self-focus is extremely low and this is generally interpreted as an indication of a diminished self-concept. In contrast to her chosen occupation and her assertion that she enjoys caring for paraplegics, the psychometric data indicate that she has less interest in and understanding of other people than the average person in her reference group and that she has a higher than average need for interpersonal isolation. She also has a markedly diminished capacity for forming attachments. Contrary to her portrait of herself as the passive recipient of other people's agendas, the psychometric data indicate that she is typically active in her social relationships. Consistent with the indication of a diminished self-concept is the finding that she is insecure and needs to justify herself to others.

Sarah's personal and interpersonal difficulties notwithstanding, it is her cognitive processing that presents the biggest liability for her adoptive functioning. To begin, she attempts to organize her thinking less frequently than the average members of her reference group (who do so less frequently than the average adult) and is not very successful even when she does so. Her tendency to back away from complexity, oversimplify and deny reality is so extreme that no one in the reference group is comparable. The capacity of her rose colored glasses is so dense that she fails to read situations accurately more than half of the time. (Again, no one in the reference group has reality testing that is as impaired as hers.) Sarah is not suffering from a psychotic disorder. The indicators of such a disorder are within normal perceptions. But Sarah imposes such an idiosyncratic perspective on her perceptions that they are like no one else's in the reference group. Even when the situation is simple and straightforward she fails to view it from a conventional perspective. When the situation is not colored by emotion her ability to read it accurately improves considerably, but remains below the average for her peers.

INTERVIEW WITH SARAH:

The allegations of the complaint were reviewed with Sarah and she was given an opportunity to correct any misinformation and/or give her version of the events.

In response to paragraph eight she pointed out that D weighed five pounds 14 ounces, not five pounds four ounces, and her version jibes with the birth record. She acknowledges that he tested positive for opiates. She does not remember the circumstances that caused her to consult a physician prior to delivery, but recalls that he prescribed a three to five-day regimen of methadone and it was during that time that she went into labor. Sarah knows that D was released into her care with stipulations and acknowledges that she did not keep subsequent appointments, but points out that she was on bed rest because of low iron and post-natal complications. She claims to have kept DYFS informed about her status.

At the time she got arrested for shoplifting, she and D's father were looking for work in Jersey City when their car broke down. It was Memorial Day weekend and there were no social service agencies to help them. They spent their money on a motel and when six-month-old D needed formula, she attempted to steal it and got caught. (T had been arrested some days before on an unrelated shoplifting charge). D had been left at the motel in the care of "I." When T, who was repairing their car, found out about the arrests, he took D from I and brought him to the truck stop where he worked. His friend "M" may have been the "bum" referred to by Officer S. The "rats" were actually three kittens. The "trailer" had been converted into living quarters for the two men. They may have been drinking to celebrate Memorial Day. D was given voluntarily to DYFS who refused to return him when the couple was released the next day. After their car was fixed they returned to the shore area without him. She acknowledges that she tested positive for opiates a few days later, but says that she had a prescription for migraine medication.

She acknowledges that she did not keep her counseling appointments through June 9th, but says she attended thereafter. She was arrested, but was released on her own recognizance after she refused to be a police informant. Although she did not deny shoplifting charges she did alert the DYFS worker that she could be charged with other crimes she did not commit because her identification papers had been stolen.

She refused treatment at Surbrugg Memorial Hospital because she had already completed an inpatient program and was an outpatient at a Hampton Hospital satellite in Toms River. Most important, she claims to have been using only prescribed medication and not illicit drugs. According to Sarah she obtained second opinions at her expense for two certified evaluators: Mr. K. and Mr. L., both of whom supported her contention that she required only outpatient counseling. Reportedly DYFS rejected these reports as "not creditable".

She did miss visits because she had just been in an auto accident, had a broken neck and was in a "halo". She denied meeting Ms. A, but says she communicated with a supervisor. Z and she were in the same accident, were on the same type of medication, but did not share. She did become angry with the DYFS worker, but not because of denial of benefits. Rather, the AFDC office had told her that DYFS had told them that she would not be getting D back and had not given her any conditions that would lead to his return. She did not deny her addiction, but did assert that she was not actively using illicit drugs at the time. She does not recall being agitated, but does recall having breathing difficulty while visiting D because of her "halo". She acknowledges difficulty with her probation officer because "...he intimidated me on a sexual level" and says he was later arrested for sexual misconduct. She acknowledges that she may have missed ten of 16 visits with D and points out that she was incapacitated from July of 1994 to December of 1994 when her "halo" was removed. She denies that she failed to contact the supervisory agency. But Sarah volunteered that there was more to it than that:

"If I had seen D I would have just taken him and ran. I would have been in a heck of a lot of trouble—more than I am now. I was fighting a losing battle. I would take two steps forward and they would push me three back. I would request things (e.g. pictures of D) and they didn't give me anything."

In response to the summary allegations, Sarah replied that she stabilized her living arrangements in May of 1995 when she moved in with a "friend". Her contacts have been irregular because of her injuries. She has sought treatment through Alcoholics Anonymous and has been drug free since April of 1995. She has had no new arrests since April of 1995.

Toward the end of the evaluation, I asked Sarah why she thought she had led such a self-defeating life. She blamed it on drugs: "When I don't use drugs I don't get in trouble. That's the bottom line". But why did she continue to re-involve herself with the substances that had brought her so much pain? Sarah explained that "L" who had a wife and two kids... at the time he was carrying on an affair with her mother had very probably—she could not evoke clear memories—sexually molested her when she was a preschooler. She believes that her mother knew this based on some letters the mother sent to her years later. Nevertheless, the mother left her husband, married him and bore him four children. Over the last five years inchoate memories of L began surfacing, but she tried to suppress them. Then, probably in 1993, L called to say he was sorry as this was a part of his then current treatment. Sarah recounts it:

> "At that point I knew something happened, but I didn't want to hear it. I didn't want him saying he's sorry. You're sorry and you're a grown man, I was a three-year old girl. I didn't know how to deal with it. I didn't know how to ask for help."

She then recalled how she would have sick feelings when her husband J would approach her sexually, but at the time she had not connected them with the earlier events. She believes that it was the pain that drove her to drug use and to the crimes that she committed to support it, but she distanced herself from the actual criminal activity:

> "I have a hard time looking now that I ever did any of that, the shoplifting. I'm one of the most honest people there is. I can't believe I got busted for shoplifting. I never even took anything from a store. Even in here I don't break rules."

She talked at length about how she would get "out of control," get arrested, "get cleaned up," stay abstinent for a while and then begin the cycle again. Eventually she indicated that she had said all that she needed to and we concluded the interview by mutual agreement.

DISCUSSION:

Sarah was evaluated in an effort to determine if she has the psychological capacity to parent her two-year-old son who has not been in here care since he was six months old. Her psychological profile can be summarized as follows. She is of average or better intelligence. She is not psychotic. She has a history of depressive episodes going back at least 13 years and probably longer. These have alternated with periods of high energy when she required little sleep, which raises the possibility of a longstanding bipolar disorder that has not been diagnosed or properly treated. The depression may be the result of the alleged sexual abuse or it may have originated in an even earlier unsatisfying relationship with her mother. Much of her drug involvement can be explained as an attempt at self-medication. What is not explained by this formulation is Sarah's extremely poor judgment regarding her own best interests and the welfare of her children.

She conceived a child out-of-wedlock when she was in her mid-teens, then married the child's father who was five years older, but manifestly irresponsible from the start. Nevertheless, she remained with him eight years and was introduced to heroin drugs during that time. After freeing herself from that relationship she was lucky enough to meet and to marry a stable man with a good paying job and had a second child with him. He later divorced her because of her continuing drug use. She then became involved with Z, conceived a third child, continued an unstable lifestyle characterized by drug use and petty crime and lost her newborn within six months to child protective services. This is the kind of maladaptive behavior that would be predicted by the psychometric findings.

Sarah's ability to read situations accurately and therefore her ability to respond to them productively is extremely impaired. She says that is had been "only the last five years" that this has occurred, but my arithmetic puts it closer to ten when she accepted heroin from her first husband. A variety of interventions have been offered to her including inpatient drug treatment which she called "successful," yet by her own statement she continued to use drugs and commit crime through April of 1995, almost a year after she had lost D. If Sarah were capable of learning from experience, certainly the loss of her third child would have stopped her from being "out of control". Sarah's distorted view of relationships; her emotional distancing and diminished capacity to form attachments further aggravate her difficulty getting along in life.

The historical and current evidence leads me to belief that D has been and will continue to be harmed when he is in her care. I do not believe that she has the capacity to cease harming him in spite of her expressed intention to do so. Her liability in this area is peculiar to her own psychology and is not the result of cultural or environment is advantage. I can find no basis for recommending that D be placed back in her care.

FORENSIC ASSESSMENT:

Sarah displays a very high degree of what can be described as criminality of the addictive along with mental-emotional disturbance (1). Not every substance abuser who engages in a pattern of extremely irresponsible behavior is necessarily out of control; but, in this case, Sarah does appear to be out of control, in her criminality being explained by her substance abuse. Fortunately, the psychologist made the right decision in not recommending that D be placed back in Sarah's care. Unfortunately, however, there are far too many cases where incorrect decisions are made by court appointed psychologists and therapists (2).

The clinical psychologist reporting upon this case verbally relayed some forensic indicators to me as a result of his further acquainting himself with my classification and diagnostic system of forensic assessment. Since these indicators are not contained in his written report, however, I have decided not to comment upon them. Forensic assessment along with all other assessments in the justice system should be based upon reported and open documentation. This will enable us to analyze critique and refine our assessments ... clinical and otherwise ... with more scientific scrutiny. What's essential in terms of both ethics and science, is that all assessments in the justice system be open to scientific research. The confidentiality protection that is used to hinder research is more a protection for the unscientific nature of much clinical psychology than it is for the protection of a client.

CASE 2: JANE

PSYCHOLOGICAL EVALUATION
NAME: Jane, Age 27

REASON FOR EVALUATION:
The evaluation was requested by the case manager pursuant to a court order to assess the Client's psychological capacity to parent her daughters: As, three and An, two, who have been raised in alternative care. The Division is seeking to terminate the Client's parental rights in order to free As and An for adoption and she is contesting the action.

BASIS OF EVALUATION:
Rorschach Psychodiagnostic   Interview with the Client
Complaint for Guardianship by DAG

BACKGROUND INFORMATION:
The following information was provided by Jane and has not been verified.
Jane was born and raised in Trenton. Her mother was only 16 when she delivered her and spent six months in the hospital because of complications. Jane was cared for by her maternal grandmother, bonded with her and was "spoiled rotten" by the time her birth mother reentered the family home. The two women shared in her care from then on. Her birth father was a marginal figure in her life. She avoided him because he was often drunk in public, which embarrassed her. Her mother married another man when Jane was about three and he proved to be "the father I didn't have". The couple separated when Jane was about six but the stepfather continued to be positive influence in her life. A brother, seven years younger, was born of her mother's union with that man and a brother four years younger has a different father. Her grandmother died when Jane was in her early 20s. Her mother is in her early 40s and they have regular contact. The older of the two brothers is out of contact and "probably in the streets somewhere..." The younger brother earned his high school equivalency diploma after some academic difficulties and is now employed.

Jane earned her high school diploma in Florida during the 18 months that she lived there while caring for a sick relative. During that time she became a certified nurse's assistant. She has been employed as bookkeeper in both the state government and a private corporation. Her longest period of continuous employment was two and one-half years as a private security guard. She was laid off when the company lost a large contract. She was employed most recently eight months ago wiring electrical harnesses. She left when she was pregnant.

Jane has never been married. She has produced four children by her unions with four different men. K, who is now eight, was born when she was 18 and has been raised by Jane's maternal aunt. As and An, who are subjects of the complaint, were born five and six years later respectively. T is five months old and is in the same foster home as his sisters. With the exception of As's father (who married someone else), Jane did not anticipate a permanent relations with any of the men because "they had nothing going for themselves" and none takes responsibility for his offspring. Jane did not protect herself against sexually transmitted disease because she considered the men "boyfriends". She did not use birth control pills because they made her sick. None of the pregnancies was planned - "All of a sudden I would pop up pregnant" - and she does not believe in abortion. K and A were born with drugs in their systems. The other children were not.

Jane began smoking marijuana when she was 17 and was smoking cocaine about a year later with "the wrong people". At age 22 she "just got tired of it," stopped, then started again after her grandmother's death. (She was vague about the length of her abstinence referring to it both as three years and as one year.) She has not participated in detoxification or in rehabilitation. She last imbibed in November of 1998 because she found out that she was pregnant with T and did not want him to be exposed to drugs in utero.

Jane represented that she has no juvenile criminal record. She was convicted of possession with intent to distribute drugs about three years ago. She served 16 months of a four year sentence at the Edna Mahan Correction Center, was paroled, remained free for about a year and was re-incarcerated for violating her parole by not reporting. (Jane said that she did not feel well enough to travel to the parole office because she was pregnant with T.) Jane denied any other arrests and/or convictions. She does not have a driver's license and denied any record of motor vehicle violations.

At the present time, Jane is in the seventh month of her incarceration at the Mercer County Correction Center. She participates in a substance abuse support group when it is available. There are not other activities offered. She works in the institution's kitchen. She anticipates her release in June or at the latest in August. After that she will live with a friend with whom she is not romantically involved. She can depend on her mother and her aunt (who is raising K) for support. She intends to enroll in a county sponsored culinary arts program. She cannot pursue her nurse's assistant certification because of her history of drug involvement. She has no romantic interest at this time.

OBSERVATIONS AND IMPRESSIONS:

Jane was interviewed in a section of the prison library under distant supervision. She was dressed in an orange T-shirt, pants and athletic shoes. Her hair was pulled back. She had a picture I.D. bracelet. Makeup and jewelry were not apparent. She is of average height (5'6"), overweight (189 lbs.) and without apparent physical handicaps. She said that she had glasses but did not generally wear them. There was nothing remarkable about her posture, stance or gait on brief observation. She displayed no unusual speech patterns or mannerisms. She was cooperative and made adequate eye contact.

Jane's intelligence appears to be within normal limits. She was oriented in person, place and time. She was alert and able to focus and sustain her attention. She understood the reason for the evaluation and appeared capable of defending herself against allegations. Her memory for both recent and remote events is serviceable. Her associations were rapid and relevant. There was no evidence of psychotic processes.

Jane said she was asthmatic and had bronchitis. An inhaler is not available. She takes iron for anemia. She smokes one package of cigarettes daily while confined but less than ten when she is free. She is intolerant of lactose but otherwise has no dietary problems. She has no problem sleeping and feels rested in the morning. She denied psychological symptoms in the form of obsessions, compulsions, phobias and psychotic episodes. She further denied both suicidal and homicidal ideation.

Jane's mood was appropriately sober for the circumstances. She displayed a normal range and intensity of emotion. Her control was adequate. If she attempted to obstruct communication or dissemble I could not detect it. The nature and scope of the procedure as well as the limits of confidentiality were reviewed with Jane and she agreed to cooperate. The impression was that she was capable of producing valid and reliable findings.

PSYCHOMETRIC FINDINGS:

After being coded by hand Jane's responses to the Rorschach test were tabulated and analyzed using the Rorschach Interpretation Assistance Program. Some of the phrasing in this report overlaps with the computer generated statements. However what has been highlighted and the emphasis given to it are my responsibility. The number and variety of responses made by Jane constitute an interpretively useful record. The most salient feature of the record is her pronounced deficiency in coping capacity. The analysis of her psychological organization and functioning shall proceed from this finding.

Jane exists in a chronic state of disequilibrium. This is not because of an excessive amount of stress but because of a dearth of resources for dealing with. Both her capacity for objective analysis and her capacity to marshal her emotions are diminished in comparison to the majority of the people to whom they are compared. She functions best in structured settings and is vulnerable to loss of control when she has to rely on her own Capacity. She tends to gratify her urges impulsively without sufficient attention to the long-range consequences of her actions. Although this helps to keep her subjective experience of stress to a minimum it sets her up for later difficulties. As mentioned above her emotions are not readily available to enliven her behavior. Nor are they consistent in the way they influence her thinking. She may be too constricted when more spontaneity is in order and too labile when a more dispassionate response is appropriate. The insurgence of emotions increases her proneness to lose her self-control.

Jane's self-esteem is diminished in comparison to other adults. She is not very introspective and social interactions (both positive and negative) have contributed significantly to her sense of who she is. Jane is interested in other people. She expects positive interactions and is amenable to close relationships. However, she lacks social maturity and prefers a passive role in her relationships. The focus on her personal needs and agenda's tends to make her less sensitive to the needs and agendas of others, particularly those who are dependent on her.

Jane has not developed a preferred approach to problem solving. In and of itself this is not abnormal or even that unusual: about 20 percent of the population functions in the same way. It bears mention because individuals without a preferred approach are less efficient problem solvers and tend to have more adjustment problems than individuals who have developed an approach. She has a marked tendency to narrow and oversimplify that which she is willing to consider relevant. She tends to process what she takes in a hasty, unorganized manner, which ignores nuance and subtlety. Her thinking is neither complex nor sophisticated by adult standards. Together these processing liabilities create chronic and pervasive problems in her ability to read situations accurately.

INTERVIEW WITH THE CLIENT:

The allegations of the Complaint for Guardianship were reviewed with Jane and she was given the opportunity to correct any misinformation and/or give version of events. Jane said that she had read the document and was familiar with its contents..... Jane said she smoked cocaine daily while she was pregnant with K, but explained she did not know that she was carrying her until the eighth month. Jane lived with the aunt who had custody of the newborn and participated in K's care. She acknowledged that As also tested positive, but denied that she used drugs while pregnant. She believes that the cocaine entered her bloodstream through the pores in her skin because she handled it regularly as part of her drug dealing.

Jane was self-supporting prior to her arrest but moved in with her aunt because her apartment was substandard. She was arrested and had been in the Edna Mahan Correction Center for a month at the time An was born. An was therefore placed in foster care with As, who the aunt had surrendered after Jane was arrested. Jane was released in November of 1997 and has not been notified that the sisters' cases had been transferred to the Adoption Resource Center one month earlier. She did not receive the letter informing her about visitation and come in on her own to request it. She failed to confirm the April visit because she was not familiar with the procedures. She did not attend subsequent or a court hearing because she was incarcerated. She did receive the letter informing her of the move toward guardianship but did not understand its implication.

Jane stipulated to the first prong of the summary allegation which alleges a lack of contact with her daughters but said there was a mitigating factor. "Basically it's not my fault because I was locked up most of the time." She denied the second prong, which alleges a lack of contact with the Division, "I have called and spoke to (the case manager from the Burlington County District Office) because they're the ones whose got my kids". She said that it was her understanding that the Adoption Resource Center was under the District Office. In response to the third prong, which alleges that she has not fulfilled her parental obligations, Jane said that it was because her lawyers had not assisted her in arranging for the court ordered evaluations.

In closing, I asked Jane if there was anything else that she wanted to say on behalf of preserving her parental rights. Jane said that she was not asking for physical custody at this time because she knew she would not be in a position to care for the girls when she was released, "First thing I have to do is get a job and get me established so my kids will have a place to come home to". She is asking for six months to prove that she can be an adequate mother.

"I didn't have four kids to abandon them, give them up for adoption. I know I have made a lot of mistakes but I really want a second chance. I see a lot of people out there who has been on drugs worse than me and they got their kids. DYFS can keep a close check on them. I'm older now and I want to be the one to support them, do the things I haven't done for years. I'll do whatever (the court) wants."

Discussion:

Jane has been evaluated in an effort to determine if she has the psychological capacity to parent her preschool daughters who have been raised in alternative care. Jane's early history is of the kind so often heard from mothers who are in jeopardy of losing their parental rights. According to her own statements she grew up in a loving home and did not suffer material hardships. She earned a high school diploma. She has a way of earning a living and has in fact been employed at several points during her 20s. But Jane has also exercised some very poor judgment. Her first pregnancy was accidental and could be explained by her youth, but Jane then went on to deliver three more children when she was in her 20s because she did not believe she could become pregnant after delivering her first child. She considered the fathers "boyfriends" and did not intend to make a life with any of them. She used drugs intermittently during the years of her child bearing and sold them, which resulted in her incarceration. She was released after serving only a small part of a four-year sentence then violated her parole by failing to report. Even now she does not seem to fully appreciate the seriousness of what she has (and has not) done, "I know people worse than me....". Her psychological profile as revealed through the Rorschach test is highly congruent and would predict much of her actual behavior.

Jane exists in a continual state of disequilibrium because she has never developed the thinking skills to solve problems that most adults take in stride. Nor does she have an adult level of emotional control. She can function well in structured settings, such as her present one, but when left on her own action can be expected to follow quickly on the heels of impulse. Because she lacks the ability to read situations accurately and to plan for contingencies her life is a series of crisis. She gravitates toward people but values relationships primarily to the degree that they meet her needs rather than finding satisfaction in nurturing others.

Neither her conduct vis-à-vis the children nor her present psychological evidence provides any basis for recommending that Jane be given the primary responsibility for raising a child. She has too much work to do on her personal development first. Nor is Jane asking that she be given such responsibility – at least not at this time. She is asking only that she be given a "second chance" to show what she can do now that she is in the right frame of mind. I do not know whether Jane will develop the judgment, reasoning capacity and emotional control to be an adequate parent in the future but I do know that the time to develop those capacities will require several years and not the six months she envisions to get herself "established".

FORENSIC ASSESSMENT:

Jane can be forensically classified as displaying extreme forensic denial. In a denial response analogous to an alcoholic's denial of "I can handle my drinking," Jane's response of "I know people worse than me" is classic in demonstrating the process of forensic denial rationalization. Her criminal rationality is that she knows herself not to be as criminal or as bad, as others know her to be. Her rationalization is such that she exhibits a high degree of denial to support and feed what the psychologist describes as very poor judgment.... to the extreme. Her emotional control is so pathologically unstructured that the psychologist correctly concludes that he does not know whether she will develop the judgment, reasoning capacity and emotional control to be an adequate parent in the future.

Forensically, however, her criminal denial rationalization is highly structured; and it serves as a forensics enabler in supporting her irresponsible and criminal choices. After her first supposedly accidental pregnancy, she chooses to deliver three more children... with no regard to her responsibility to those children or to the society that she's delivered them into. She chooses to use drugs intermittently during her childbearing years, as well as to sell drugs. After being released upon serving only a small part of a four-year sentence, she chooses to violate her parole by failing to report.

In rationalizing all her choices, she consistently assigns responsibility to someone other than herself. Others are deemed to be at fault for all her failures, and even her four pregnancies are not deemed to be her fault. Incredibly, in rational terms, but quite credibly in the rationalization of forensic denial, she reasons that she couldn't believe she could have become pregnant after delivering her first child. She considers the various fathers of her children to be boyfriends with no expectation or intention on her part to make a life with them.

Although her case points towards extreme mental-emotional pathology, the forensic pathology of denying responsibility for her choices enabled Jane to continue to act upon her mental and emotional deficiencies. Just as the first step in any AA (Alcoholics Anonymous) meeting is to directly address and overcome denial, in acknowledging ones' alcoholism to others, Jane needs to be taught how to take that first step in overcoming her forensic denial. Therefore, forensic counseling along with addiction and psychological counseling is called for.

CASE 3: MARIE

PSYCHOLOGICAL EVALUATION

REASON FOR EVALUATION:
The evaluation was requested by the case manager pursuant to court order to assess the Client's psychological capacity to parent her three children: Child One, 14; Child Two, 13 and Child Three, 5. The Division is seeking to terminate the Client's parental rights in order to free the children for adoption and she is contesting the action.

BASIS OF EVALUATION:
Rorschach Psychodiagnostic   Interview with the Client
Complaint for Guardianship by DAG

BACKGROUND INFORMATION:
The following history was proved by Marie and has not been verified.
She was born and raised in Trenton in an intact family. Her father was about nine years older than her mother. He was employed as an installer of floor covering and was also a minister. Her mother was a teacher of home economics. She is the youngest of six siblings. Her brothers and sisters range in age from their early 60s to late 40s. There was no substance abuse, domestic violence or criminal activity while Marie was growing up. Her birth father died of cancer in 1990 at the age of 80. Her mother died of heart failure in 1984 at the age of 66. Two of her siblings are deceased. One of her sisters is a minister; another is a buyer for a trucking company, her brother is a baker. The brother lives locally and she sees him occasionally. The sisters live out of state and she does not have contact with them.

After graduating high school, Marie attended college with the goal of becoming a surgical nurse but quit after a year when she discovered that she could not stand the sight of blood. She subsequently earned an associates degree in business management and a certificate in computer operations. Over the last 20 years her longest period of continuous employment was eight years in the cottage life department of the Skillman residential facility. She had advanced to a supervisory position and had tenure but quit because, "I got tired of going out there". She has also held positions in domestic sales (three years) and in a meat retailer (six years). Her employment ended when the retail store closed. She quit the meat retailer to care for her father when he became ill. For the last three months she has been a pharmacist assistant in a drug store.

Marie has never been married. Child One resulted from her union with Mr. F and was an unplanned pregnancy. Marie wanted to make a life with Mr. F and he could not commit to the relationship and takes on responsibility for his son. Child Two was a "planned" pregnancy from her union with Mr. A with whom she did not expect to make a life. Mr. A was an intravenous drug user and died of AIDS. Child Three was a planned pregnancy from her union with Mr. H who is 12 years her senior. She expected to have a long-term relationship with him but he deserted her when she was two months pregnant. Marie said that she had miscarried a child prior to conceiving Child Three. She mentioned no other children.

Marie denied any history of alcohol dependence. She began smoking "crack" cocaine in her early 20s at the suggestion of some friends and it became her drug of choice for the next ten years. I asked Marie why she had begun imbibing cocaine at such a late age. She replied "I have no idea. I can't explain that to you, maybe because I was alone and trying to raise children". But she assured me that being a mother did not make her feel overwhelmed. Marie has never completed a detoxification or rehabilitation program, "I think they're really stupid. It's up to you to stop". (She buttressed her statements by adding that she knew of people who had been through such programs and did not benefit. She stopped on her own in the summer of 1997 because, "I knew I had to get myself together. I could bullshit them (i.e. DYFS) but I could not bullshit the court". She has maintained her abstinence through the present time.

At first Marie denied having any criminal history then admitted that she had been arrested for trespassing on the property of the Trenton Police station. According to Marie she, her children and another woman were taking a shortcut from the motel where she was living to a soup kitchen when they were confronted by the police officers. Marie thought, "This is a city. I pay taxes, so what?" and kept walking. The charges were later dropped. Marie also admitted that she was incarcerated for 38 days and ordered to make restitution for welfare fraud. She explained that she was working and collecting benefits because, "I wanted to make sure my children had the best of everything and wanted to still smoke (cocaine)". Marie did not admit to any other criminal history and demurred on the question of present wants or warrants. She has not had a valid driver's license for an unspecified never paid ticket since 1989 "because I thought my job (Thomas Edison State College) should have paid my ticket. It was their fault. They should have had a parking space for me".

At the present time, Marie is living with her cousin and the cousin's baby in the home of her aunt who is in Texas. She is employed six days per week, eight to ten hours daily. For recreation she watched TV: doctor shows, detective shows, "Since I've been a child I've been at TV freak". For the last four years she has been romantically involved with an older man who is a former drug user and who now works as a cook. She did not know what relationship or responsibilities he had to his own children, "We don't speak of his children, only about mine. It has to be that way till I get mine back". She is pragmatic about their relationship. "I've had relationships longer than this and they did not become permanent." She attended the Heartland Clinic for all day sessions for about a month before she began her present employment but could not tell me the focus of the intervention; "You would have to ask them. I never understood it myself". At present, "I go when I think I need someone to talk to". She last saw her children about two years ago informally. There are no supervised visits at present.

OBSERVATIONS AND IMPRESSIONS:

Marie was transported to the Central ARC office by a DYFS case-worker. She is of average heights (5'5"), overweight (210 lbs.) and without apparent physical handicaps. She wears glasses for reading and watching TV. She is missing some teeth. She was dressed in a white T-shirt, white pants and sandals. There were four rings and a watch on her left hand and one ring on her right. A purse hung from her shoulder. Her speech was rapid and pressured and not well articulated. Her attitude was hostile. Her manner of relating was both guarded and evasive. Her eye contact was adequate. There was nothing remarkable about her posture, stance or gait on brief observation. Marie's intelligence appears to be within normal limits and possibly above average. She was oriented in person, place and time. She was alert and able to focus and sustain her attention. She understood the reason for the evaluation and appeared capable of defending herself against the allegations. Her memory for both recent and remote was serviceable although selective. Her associations were rapid and relevant. She tended to talk around issues and switch topics mid-paragraph. There was not evidence of psychotic processes. If she had any insight into her own role in her present difficulties she did not express it.

Marie said her joints ache following an auto accident in February of 1996, but that she was otherwise in good health. She reported no problems eating or sleeping. She denied any psychological symptoms in the forms of obsessions, compulsions, phobias and psychotic episodes. She admitted to thoughts of suicide by ingesting pills after her children were taken but could not remember the months or the year.

Marie's mood was one of anger and annoyance at the way she had been treated by social service agencies. Sometimes she was amused by their incompetence. She was cavalier about her own actions. She was tearful at the end. Her control was adequate for the purposes of the evaluation. The nature and scope of the procedures as well as the limits of confidentiality were reviewed with Marie and she agree to cooperate. The impression was that she was capable for producing valid and reliable findings.

PSYCHOMETRIC FINDINGS:

After being coded by hand, Marie's responses to the Rorschach were tabulated and analyzed using the Rorschach Interpretation Assistance Program. Some of the phrasing in this report overlaps with the computer generated statements. However, what has been highlighted and the emphasis given to it are my responsibility. The number and variety of responses made by Marie constitute an interpretively useful record. The most salient feature of the record is the elevated Coping Deficit Index. The analysis of her psychological organization and functioning shall proceed from this finding.

In purely arithmetic terms, Marie is in equilibrium. In actuality her cognitive resources are far below those of the average adult and she has no measurable capacity to draw on her emotions to fuel her goal directed behavior. What creates the spurious equilibrium is her stress level, which is unrealistically low by adult standards. How she maintains it at such a low level and the price she pays for it are discussed below in the paragraph dealing with cognitive processing.

Marie's proneness to become emotionally aroused is about the same as other adults. However, she is quite concerned about modulating and controlling her emotional displays and tends to keep her feelings at a peripheral level when thinking through problems. She does give indication of the ability to recognize her feelings when necessary. Social interactions have contributed significantly to Marie's sense of who she is and her self-esteem appears diminished in comparison to other adults.

She produced mixed findings regarding her interpersonal perceptions and relations. On the one hand she appears interested in other people and is amenable to close relationships. On the other hand she does not anticipate positive relationships and tends to remain on the periphery of group interaction. The apparent contradiction can be resolved when one understands that Marie is less socially mature than one would expect at her age and that she is more likely to manifest dependency behavior in her relationships. She expects others to be tolerant of her needs and demands and is less sensitive to the needs of others. Her naiveté regarding her interpersonal relations makes her vulnerable to rejection and to dissatisfaction in her social life.

To the degree that she has a preference Marie prefers an objective approach to problem solving and tends to keep her emotions on the periphery. However, preference is not the same as capacity and Marie has considerable difficulty with the way she processes information. Although Marie spends considerable time scanning the environment she narrows and over-simplifies that she is willing to consider relevant. The processing of what she takes in is done in a hasty and haphazard manner, which neglects subtlety and nuance. Although these tactics keep her stress level low and help to maintain her equilibrium they undermine her ability to read situations accurately and create considerable distortion in her thinking. When her emotions well up they further hinder her ability to think clearly.

INTERVIEW WITH THE CLIENT:

The allegations of the Complaint were reviewed with Marie and she was given the opportunity to correct any misinformation and/or give her version of events.

Marie admitted that she used cocaine while she was pregnant with Child Three but denied knowing that it would hurt her daughter in utero. She reported that Child Three tested positive for cocaine at birth but denied that she herself did because she had stopped imbibing at some unstated time before delivery. Marie was laughing when she called for an ambulance and therefore the person receiving her call did not believe that she was in labor. Child Three was born at home as a result. Marie thinks that the hospital was negligent.

Marie identified her "friend" as child Three's godmother, denied that the woman had made the statements attributed to her and said that Ms. J was herself a drug addict.

Marie acknowledged that there were unpaid bills and taxes levied on the house where she was living and said these were left over from her father's occupancy and should have been paid by her brother who was in charge of the family finances. Regarding the allegedly substandard conditions of the house, Marie explained that her father did his own work and that the house had fallen into disrepair when he became ill. The house was condemned but Marie was living in it two years later. She explained "the house was condemned" because I chose for it to be. The guy did that for me because he was a friend of mine".

After the condemnation, Marie and her children were moved to a motel but she was evicted a few months later because she did not attend a meeting to review her case. Marie said that no one from welfare came to transport her to that meeting. She stayed with friends but had to leave because the home was overcrowded. She lived with "H" but had to leave because he was cruel to Child One. She denied being "passed out" during the day in another residence. After that she lived in motels but was evicted because DYFS would not pay her rent, "It was nothing of my doing." She then obtained her own living quarters but was evicted a few months later for non-payment of rent. She stayed with a friend and was getting her meals at a soup kitchen. She ended up in a motel again with the help of DYFS and the children were placed in foster care the next day. Visitation did not start for almost two months after the children were placed and Marie laid the blame for this to the slow action of DYFS. Marie remained without her own living quarters and was out of contact with DYFS for lengthy periods. Marie explained, "they were not allowing me to see my children so I just didn't...If they know where I was why didn't they come or call. They had the number and address".

Marie tested positive for cocaine and admitted that she was still using drugs almost two years after her children were placed. I asked her why she continued when she know that it would keep her separated from her children. Marie responded: "Again, you as a psychologist can go and state that maybe she should have gotten deeper into drugs or something to relieve the pain. People go that way also".

She then told me that that was not her motivation. "If I had been that type of weak person I would have killed myself." Regardless of her addiction Marie asserted that she had never left her children alone or neglected them.

"Whatever I did my children were never in harms way. They were always fed and they were always clothed. I never mistreated my children." Marie signed a service agreement in which she committed to attend sessions at Children's Home Society but it was not a beneficial experience. Marie agreed that she was not interested in the program: "The only reason I was going there was because I wanted to see my children. I wasn't going for myself -I don't need anyone to teach me how to be a mother".

Marie missed visits with her children because she failed to confirm them one day in advance as required. Marie explained:

"I told them face to face 48 hours before. Why is 48 hours different from 24 hours? I'm telling you what I told them. I don't have a phone either."

Marie eventually "quit" the program because "D was a liar. I wanted the whole case to get out of her office because I did not want to be bothered with her anymore".

Marie admitted that she had missed planning sessions but said that she had not been notified. She claimed that she had not been notified when the case was transferred to the ARC and later to guardianship proceedings. She admitted that she had threatened to kidnap her children; "I know their address, their telephone number and the school they go to. I can walk up any day and snatch them". But she assured me, "I'm gonna get them back through the right channels". Marie denied that she was planning on leaving the country, "That's crazy! I don't know anybody out of the country".

Marie responded to the first prong of the summary allegation regarding her chronic homelessness by denying it - "I moved exactly one time in the last four years: from 248 Brunswick to 326 Wayne"- and added that she had found living quarters but had given them up because DYFS would not return the children. She denied the instability alleged by the second prong, "I've had jobs. I couldn't work. It's not my fault that a car hit me". Regarding her addiction, which is alleged in the third prong, Marie did not deny it but added, "How would they know? They've never seen me doing drugs". Marie admitted that she had not cooperated with the services offered and had been prevented from visiting her children as a consequence but did not agree that visitation should be contingent upon accepting those services.

In closing, I asked Marie if she had anything additional she wanted to say on behalf of preserving her parental rights. She replied:

"I want my children back. I have always loved m children. I never did anything to hurt my children. I never would do anything to hurt my children. Drugs are not in my life anymore. I have someone in my life who truly cares for me."

DISCUSSION:

Marie has been evaluated in an effort to determine if she has the psychological capacity to be a full time parent to her three children who have been out of her care for almost three years. The three children were born out of wedlock. Child One was not planned and the birth father deserted her. Child Two was "planned" with a man with whom she did not expect to make a life, who was an intravenous drug user and who died of AIDS. Child Three was "planned" with a man who deserted her two months into her pregnancy. I asked Marie about the wisdom of having unprotected sex in an age when there is so much publicity about sexually transmitted disease. She replied, "To be a highly intelligent, worldly aware person has nothing to do with your sex life. People in your profession have AIDS".

But what about the wisdom of having three children when you have no place to live and no means to support them? Marie assured me that she had adequate housing at the time each child was born and that the six-year chronology detailed in the Complaint amounted to nothing more than a series of financial setbacks.

Marie took no responsibility for her present state of affairs. She told me earlier in the interview, "The only reason I don't have my children is because I didn't have a place to live". She expanded on her position later on. "They can pay (somebody else) to take care of my kids but could not give me the same amount of money. If they had helped me find a job I could have gotten off welfare."

Marie did not acknowledge that she is a drug addict. "A person don't have a problem unless they chose to have a problem. I have no idea what I have. I know a person can stop anytime they chose to." And Marie is sure that what she has had no negative impact on her children, "A DYFS worker once told me that some of the best parents are drug and alcohol abusers".

Any optimism that one might have regarding her self-directed rehabilitation is dashed by her reason for doing so:

"I knew all this was coming up, what we're doing right here. I know all the steps of what they was going to do. I put myself in a position where I could defend myself. I wanted it on paper that, yes, she has done this; she has done that."

But Marie has learned one important lesson from her ordeal, "I made a mistake. I shouldn't have gotten involved with DYFS. Now I know other ways to get help. If it happened today I wouldn't go to DYFS".

Her current psychological profile, as elicited by the Rorschach, is highly congruent with the flawed logic in the above statements and with the mal-adaptive way she has lived her life. Even the ambivalence regarding her interpersonal relations is reflected in her own statement. "I used to trust people in the past. I'm not like that any more." In answer to the referring question, Marie does not demonstrate the psychological capacity to be the primary care provider for your young children. If it is true that she is no longer drug involved, is employed, has housing and has a stable relationship with another person it is to her credit. But even at this relatively tranquil juncture in her life her equilibrium is tenuous. Given her history and current psychological profile there is no realistic basis for assuming that she is going to gain the requisite capacity to parent in the future. This opinion is offered without prejudice to any relationship Marie may have with her children as I have not had the opportunity to valuate those relationships at this writing.

FORENSIC ASSESSMENT:

Marie's case reveals some similarities with, as well as distinct differences from the forensic characteristics evidenced in the previous case with Jane. While there is a strong forensic denial in both cases, Marie also displays a very strong functional rationality. The forensic or criminal functional rationality referred to is one wherein a criminal functions, quite rationally, to get what he or she wants.

Although I agree with the conclusion of the psychologist as to there being no realistic basis for assuming that Marie is going to gain the requisite capacity to parent in the future, my forensic assessment is different in analyzing the dynamics of her mental condition. Before presenting my forensic analysis, I'd like to present evidence of her forensic denial as follows:

Marie admitted using cocaine while pregnant, but denied knowing that it would hurt her daughter in utero. She asserted that she never left her children alone or neglected them, in stating "Whatever I did my children were never in harm's way; they were always fed and they were always clothed". In response to a signed agreement in which she committed herself to attend parent sessions at The Children's Home Society, she stated, "I don't need anyone to teach me how to be a mother".

As telling as her forensic denial is in demonstrating a similar pattern of forensic denial that Jane, our previous client, psychologically speaking, or offender, forensically speaking, demonstrated, what is far more salient in Marie's case is what can be described, cognitively, as her criminal functional rationality. In assessing this forensic functional rationality, I would part from the psychological diagnosis in a number of ways to include the following.

The psychologist observes:

"The Client's intelligence appears to be within normal limits and possible above average. She was oriented in person, place and time. She was alert and able to focus and sustain her attention."

"She understood the reason for the evaluation and appeared capable of defending herself against the allegations. Her memory for both recent and remote was serviceable although selective".

"Her associations were rapid and relevant. She tended to talk around issues and switch topics mid-paragraph. There was no evidence of psychotic processes. If she had any insight into her own role in her present difficulties she did not express it".

I would disagree with the concluding psychological inference of her having no insight, and I'd stress the very opposite....of her having immense insight into what's relevant to her, according to her functional rationality.

The considerable abilities that are attributed to her, in the psychologist referring to her skill at defending herself, her alertness and her ability to make rapid and relevant associations, indicate that she is quite insightful in treating herself to what she wants ...rather than wanting to be treated by a therapist.

The psychological diagnosis is often anti-opposite to the forensic diagnosis which should appear in this case. The following psychological analysis in illustrative of how the forensic dynamics of this offender are obscured, at best, and lost, at worst, in the misinterpretations that result when clinical psychological analysis is applied to cases that call for clinical forensic analysis. The clinical psychologist concludes: To the degree that she has a preference; the Client prefers an objective approach to problem solving and tends to keep her emotions on the periphery. However, preference is not the same as capacity and the Client has considerable difficulty with the way she processes information. Although the Client spends considerable time scanning the environment, she narrows and oversimplifies what she is willing to consider relevant. Her processing of what she takes in is done in a hasty and haphazard manner, which neglects subtlety and nuance. Although these tactics keep her stress low and help to maintain her equilibrium, they undermine her ability to read situations accurately and create considerable distortion in her thinking. When her emotions well up they further hinder her ability to think clearly.

Forensically, there is no evidence, whatsoever, that Marie, the offender, is now Marie, the psychological client, who has difficulty in processing information, cannot think clearly, and is unable to read situations accurately. To the contrary, she reads situations quite accurately with very clear thinking, according to her criminal functional rationality. I've already presented evidence of her calculated forensic denial; and, now, allow me to present evidence of her clear thinking and quite able forensic functional rationality. This evidence, ironically, appears in the clinical psychologist's report.

His report states that Marie not only admitted that she had threatened to kidnap her children, but that she went further, in adding, "I know their address, their telephone number and the school they go to".

In making this statement, Marie is letting us know that she has the ways and the means, as well as the intent, to achieve her objective. This is a classic example of a calculating clear thinking, functional rationality functioning in a way that better enables one to implement one's criminal intent. As evidenced here, her functional rationality provides the criminal means to her criminal intent; and by no means is it in any way dysfunctional, in demonstrating any inability to think clearly, or to read situations accurately. Rather than being unrealistic, or unthinking or unclear, Marie reveals a quite able, clear and realistic functional rationality in getting what she wants.

The error of most psychological and psychiatric diagnosis in dealing with the functional rationality of most criminals, who display this rationality to a greater extent and higher degree than other criminal rationalities (1) lies in the assumption that criminality is irrational.

In the therapeutic community's misunderstanding of the criminal rationalities involved in criminality, the helping professions of psychology and psychiatry have applied a quite UNHELPFUL medical model of pathology for treating criminal rationalities as irrational. The failure of these medical model approaches in treating criminality is not due to irrational criminal clients, but rather, it results from irrational therapeutic diagnosis in treating a criminal rationality as if it's an irrationality. Therapeutic failures result from the therapists projecting their failed diagnostic process as to what is reasonable or pathological onto criminals with a quite different, but quite reasonable rationality of their own.

In reality, criminal or otherwise, criminality, in general, and the calculated lies associated with a calculating criminal rationality, in particular, are quite rational in terms of getting what one wants. The forensic functional rationality is the one particular criminal rationality most suited for enabling a criminal to accomplish his or her particular criminal objective with a particularly rational modus operandi, as to all the criminal particularities involved.

Forensically, we must say that criminal rationalities are not very nice; but, therapeutically, we must also say that it is not very nice to distort criminological analysis, in applying medical model treatment that does not apply to the criminality to be treated. Quite simply, forensic criminal pathologies are not synonymous with psychological or psychiatric pathologies. The failure to make this correct analytic distinction accounts for the failure of much criminological treatment.

The ability to read situations realistically, think clearly, and clearly defend oneself is often a concomitant of the functional rationality; and it is the very antithesis of a dysfunctional psychological or psychiatric pathology. When Marie was presented with her chronic homelessness, she immediately defended herself by stating that she'd moved only one time in four years. She further added to her defense by maintaining that she had to give up her living quarters because DYFS would not return the children. In defending herself from the allegation of joblessness, she stated, "I've had jobs; it's not my fault that a car hit me."

In reference to her proven addiction, she countered, "How would they know? They've never seen me doing drugs".

On a personal and professional note, I'd like to mention that I've spent many years moderating college student debates. The debating skills of defending oneself, making points and counter pointing against an opponent takes considerable time and practice for even the very best college students to perfect. In studying the functional rationality of criminals, I'd venture to say that many of them have developed this skill to the extent that they'd outpoint more of my college student debaters than I care to admit.

We can observe considerable mastery of this skill in the case before us. When the psychologist asked Marie about the wisdom of having unprotected sex, she replied, "People in your profession have AIDS."

Counterpoint! I would have to acknowledge as a debate moderator, in giving credit where it may not be due. One can duly note in this instance among others how the forensic functional rationality operates in defending its proponent, in providing rationalizations to deflect blame. Marie carries her rationalization process even further, in not only refusing to accept any responsibility in deflecting blame, but in redefining, for herself, what responsibility is, as her following responses in the case report indicate:

> "The Client did not acknowledge that she is a drug addict. 'A person don't have a problem unless they chose to have a problem. I have no idea what I have. I know a person can stop anytime they chose to.' And the Client is sure what she has, has had no negative impact on her children, 'A DYFS worker once told her that some of the best parents are drug and alcohol abusers.'"

Amazingly, in reference to what constitutes responsibility, but not so amazingly in reference to what constitutes a forensic functional rationality, Marie purportedly quotes an unknown DYFS worker to assert that drug and alcohol abuse can make one a better parent.

I wouldn't be surprised if there may have been a reference by some DYFS worker at some time to some person with a substance abuse problem who managed to overcome that problem in order to become a good parent. The proclivity to distort others statements to justify one's own criminality is a very common trait that can be observed here, in the case of Marie, as well as among most others with a criminal functional rationality.

The implication for treatment is that traditional therapeutic rehabilitation programs will not only not work, but, rather, they often work to the advantage of the criminal in scoring points against the therapist. The inappropriate use of medical model, therapeutic rehabilitative counseling, in therapeutically confronting a criminal with a functional rationality as a psychological client, has led to a general disregard for and a specific abandonment of treatment(3).

Obviously, the nothing works reaction is a terrible reaction in justifying no action in criminal justice; and it's a terrible substitute for not replacing inappropriate psychological treatment with appropriate forensic treatment.

It can be criminologically concluded that nothing really works, when no real forensic counseling is put to work in confronting criminal rationalities. Before we can put real forensic assessment, diagnosis, classification and treatment to work, however, inappropriate psychological assessment which doesn't work, in not confronting criminal rationalities, has to be put out of work.

Last, but not least, even when there is appropriate psychological assessment, which may be relevant in the least case scenario of a minority of specialized criminal cases, that psychological assessment is not a substitute for forensic assessment. In the minority of criminal cases, forensic counseling needs to supplement psychological counseling; and in the majority of criminal cases, it needs to replace it. Knowing the difference will make all the difference in knowing how to make forensic treatment work.

CASE 4: JOHN

PSYCHOLOGICAL EVALUATION

REASON FOR EVALUATION:
The evaluation was requested by the case manager pursuant to a court order to assess The Client's psychological capacity to parent his 11-year old son who has never been in his care. The Division is seeking to terminate The Client's parental rights in order to free the son for adoption and he is contesting the action.

BASIS OF EVALUATION:
Rorschach Psychodiagnostic   Interview with the Client
Complaint for Guardianship FG-11-15-99

BACKGROUND INFORMATION:
The following history was provided by John and has not been verified.

He was born in Trenton and raised in Mercer County. His parents were married. His mother is white. His father is African-American. His mother was employed as a lay teacher in a parochial school. His father worked in a steel mill for 25 years and toward the end of his career had a desk job. John has a brother who is 18 months older and a sister and brother who are ten and fifteen years younger respectively. His mother has never had any substance abuse problems. His father was an episodic alcoholic and began using crack cocaine in his mid-thirties. When intoxicated he was verbally and physically abusive to his wife. The parents separated (and later divorced) when John was in his early teens, because of the father's infidelity. He and his siblings were raised in a separate residence by the mother. Neither of his parents established other relationships. The father moved out of town but maintained contact. The mother became an administrator in a county office. His older brother is a correction officer. His sister is in her last year of high school and preparing for college. His brother is well adjusted and active in sports.

Academic work came easily to John but his grades suffered because of his behavior and poor attendance. He was active in sports on both the school and community levels. He attended both parochial and public schools and "messed up in all of them". He was classified as a special education student and attended county programs till he quit at 16. He has no military or vocational experience. He has held several entry-level jobs for short periods. His longest period of continuous employment was two years hauling trash. During that time he held a second job in a meat market. He quit because he, "couldn't juggle it any more between getting high, in the streets, running. It got to the point where I wouldn't even sleep because I was up all night and had to go to work at five in the morning".

John started stealing beer from the family refrigerator before he was in his teens. By 13 he was drinking on the street with older youths. He tried marijuana when he was 15 but did not like it. By his late teens he was using crack cocaine. He abstained for less than a year under pressure from a lady friend but eventually began using again and continued till he was incarcerated three years ago.

John met Ms. W. (who got him to give up crack for a while) when he was 20 and they began living together several months later. John had fathered The Son three years earlier, but did not have physical custody of him. Ms. W. had a six-month-old son, who John accepted as his own. John/Ms. W. produced a child who is almost three and a child who is five. John mentioned no other relationships or significance and acknowledged no other children.

John was arrested for the first time when he was 15 for spray painting graffiti. Over the last decade he has committed auto thefts, theft of property, assaults and armed robbery. He estimated he has been arrested 15-20 times and convicted less than ten times. He has been incarcerated on the state level three times and has been "in and out" of the county system more times than he could remember. His present offence is for multiple armed robberies, at least one of which he committed while out on bail for the others. (The $500.00 bail money was the proceeds of an earlier robbery.)

At the present time John is in the third year of an 18-year sentence with a stipulated seven-year minimum. For the last two months, he has been on "gang minimum" status and hopes to achieve full minimum in September. He represented that he has a good institutional record. He serves in the officer's dining room. He manages a basketball team and is an official at soccer games. He earned his General Educational Development (GED) diploma in 1998 and was at the top of his class. He also earned certificates in anger management, substance abuse awareness, smoking cessation and religion through a bible correspondence school. He participates in AA/NA meetings, behavior modification, group counseling and self-esteem building. His earliest possible parole date is 2002 but he could earn his way to a DOC camp and eventually to a half way house during the next two years. He has contact with family members and has visits with Ms. W. and her son who is now eight.

OBSERVATIONS AND IMPRESSIONS:

John was interviewed in what appeared to be a walk-in utility closet at the East Jersey State Prison. He is a big man (5'11", 225 lbs.) without apparent physical handicaps. His head was shaven and he had a small beard around his mouth. His arms are adorned with several tattoos among them "1/2" to signify that he is bi-racial and L to show his devotion to Ms. W. He was dressed in brown uniform, white T-shirt and athletic shoes. There was nothing remarkable about his posture, stance or gait on brief observation. He displayed no unusual speech patterns or mannerisms. He was cooperative and made adequate eye contact.

John's intelligence appears to be within normal limits. He was oriented in person, place and time. He was alert and able to focus and sustain his attention. He understood the reason for the evaluation and appeared capable of defending himself against the allegations. His memory for both recent and remote events is serviceable. His associations were rapid and relevant. There was not evidence of psychotic processes. John said he was in "great" health. Aside from occasional hay fever he has no chronic medical conditions and does not take medication on a regular basis. He is a non-smoker. He reported no problem eating or sleeping. He gets seven hours sleep nightly and feels rested. He denied psychological symptoms in the forms of obsessions, compulsions, phobias and psychotic episodes. He admitted to neither suicidal nor homicidal ideation. John's mood was appropriate sober for the circumstances. He displayed a normal range of emotions. His control was adequate for the purposes of the evaluation. His judgment has been manifestly impaired in the past but appears to be considerably improved at present. He showed insight into his own role in bringing about his present state of affairs and expressed remorse for the pain he has caused others. The nature and scope of the procedures as well as the limits of confidentiality were reviewed with John and he agreed to cooperate. The impression was that he was capable for producing valid and reliable findings.

PSYCHOMETRIC FINDINGS:

After being coded by hand, John's responses to the Rorschach test were tabulated and analyzed during the Rorschach Interpretation Assistance Program. Some of the phrasing in this report overlaps with the computer generated statements. However what has been highlighted and the emphasis given to it are my responsibility. The number and variety of responses made by John constitutes an interpretively useful record. The most salient features of the record are the elevated Depression Index and the elevated Coping Deficit Index. The analysis of his psychological organization and functioning shall proceed from these findings.

John has fewer resources available for dealing with the everyday problems of living than does the average adult. Moreover, the resources that are available are weighted on the side of emotion without any counterbalancing capacity for objective analysis. It is particularly unfortunate, therefore, that his emotional functioning is, in some respects, beyond his control. At present he is laboring under a great deal of painful affect and is expending considerable psychological energy to keep it in check. Thus he may appear wooden or emotionally constricted in situations that call for spontaneity. The other side of John is one of intensely experienced and intensely expressed emotional discharges. John is constantly challenged to keep his focus, maintain his equilibrium and resist his impulses. In situations of high demand he is vulnerable to being overwhelmed by the emotions previously held in check. Either his thinking or his behavior or both will be negatively influenced as a result.

John's self-esteem is diminished in comparison to other adults. He is not very introspective and may not have an adult level of self-understanding. The same may be said of his appreciation of other people. He has the capacity for developing close relationships. But at present he lacks an interest in other people, does not anticipate positive interactions and tends to remain in the periphery of group interactions.

John spends more time than the average adult in scanning the environment for information. However he is neither thorough nor efficient about processing the information he receives. He has a marked tendency to narrow and simplify that which he is willing to accept as relevant. He processes in a hasty and haphazard manner, which ignores nuance and subtlety. The process lacks the complexity and sophistication expected at his age. These liabilities undermine his ability to read situations accurately and create an idiosyncratic perspective, which

Interview with the Client:

The allegations of the complaint were reviewed with John and he was given an opportunity to correct any misinformation and/or give his version of events. He had read the document and was familiar with its contents. In the 70 numbered paragraphs he is mentioned less than ten times.

John acknowledges his paternity of The Son and said he had never denied it. John was incarcerated in August of 1995 but could not remember why.

He did not contact the Division regarding his son in 1996 because he believed The Son was being cared for by the birth mother's family and did not know that he was in foster care. He did not receive the letters from DYFS during 1997 and did not know he was supposed to contact them. When he was contacted in 1998 he responded as soon as he could. At that time he admitted that he had not been attentive to his son during the previous year.

John responded to the summary allegation by saying that he had had contact The Son when he was younger and saw him most recently when he was six (first prong). He has shown an interest in planning for him once he learned that The Son was in foster care (second prong).

I asked John why he had not been more attentive to his son in the earlier years before he was incarcerated. He replied that the birth mother did not encourage contact and was in fact hostile toward him but he also admitted, "We weren't close because of the sporadic life I was living".

What about that life? Why had he acted in such an antisocial and self-destructive manner for so many years. In retrospect John condemned his actions as "ridiculous" but could offer no explanation for them other that that he wanted fast money to buy more crack cocaine. He expressed remorse for the pain he had caused others, "I was a maniac out there...at my worst I was really terrible" and he thanked God that no one had been physically harmed.

In closing I asked John if there was anything else he wanted to say on behalf of preserving his parent rights. He replied:

> "I'm a different person now then when I came into jail. Now my priority is my family and my children. My son needs me and I need him. I love him although there have been many years of separation. He was my first child. I was 17 when he was born. I didn't know anything. I didn't have time for him. He didn't fit my schedule. When I leave prison I will leave as a man. I know my son needs me. I don't want to be cut out of his life."

Discussion:

John has been evaluated in an effort to determine if he has the psychological capacity to be a parent to his 11-year-old son who has never been in his care.

John's own history is hard to understand. He was raised by a "smart mother who reads all the time" and goes to church on Sunday. His siblings have turned out well according to his own statements. But John, himself, has been on an antisocial course since grade school when his mother transferred him repeatedly in the hope of finding a workable setting. There was none and John was "in the streets" full time by 16. John denied any history of mental problems but did admit that he "flipped out" (i.e. lost his self-control) during a court hearing when he was 20 and ended up in the Vroom building (now called the Forensic Psychiatric Hospital) of Trenton psychiatric Hospital for 30 days for observation. During that time he was diagnosed as an "explosive personality".

His current psychological profile, as elicited through the Rorschach, indicates a level of emotional functioning that is consistent with such a label. But the label does not explain why he has led the kind of life that he has. Explosive personalities have periods of tranquil functioning between episodes. According to his own statements John was hell bent and committed one felony after another and he was not even under the influence of cocaine at the time of the offenses.

He presents well clinically and made a favorable impression on a person to person basis. He appears to have good basic intelligence. But his resources for dealing with stresses of life are limited and he maintains his equilibrium by refusing to deal with life's complexity. This sets him up for later difficulties because the original problem is not adequately addressed. The idiosyncratic perspective from which he views life predisposes him to continual social conflict. He has a long way to go in terms of personal knowledge and appreciation of other people but he appears to have potential in both areas.

By his own admission John has neglected his son. He did not even know that the day of the evaluation was The Son's birthday. (That realization caused him visible pain). Given the history of limited contact and his present psychological profile there is no basis for recommending that he be given the responsibility of full time fatherhood. He has too much work to do on his personal development first. However, this opinion should not be construed as a recommendation that his parental rights be terminated. Such a conclusion should not be reached until other factors, including The Son's wishes, are thoroughly explored. If the court decides not to terminate John's parental rights at this time I would be happy to re-evaluate his capacity to parent at a later time when he is in a less restrictive environment to see if the clinical picture has improved.

FORENSIC ASSESSMENT:

In comparing the one male offender to the previous three female offenders, one might be tempted to express a male chauvinist sentiment to the effect that male offenders tend to be more honest than female offenders. Lest I be mistaken or misquoted as sounding like a Jesse Ventura, let me state that this offender is far more honest than most offenders Y male or female... for whatever reason. I'll leave any further speculation on this matter to Jesse and the gender specialists to comment upon....should there be a gender association or not.

Forensically, John's case can best be explained by his own explanation that he wanted fast money to buy crack cocaine. He readily acknowledges his criminality and refers to it as "ridiculous". In going even further, he expresses remorse for the pain he caused others by stating, "I was a maniac out there... at my worst I was really terrible".

In terms of denial, he denies nothing, in admitting that he was hell bent on committing one felony after another. He also acknowledges that drugs were not an excuse for his crimes, in that he was not under the influence of cocaine at the time of the offense.

After wading through the serpentine forensic denial process of so many offenders, John is a clear and welcome relief. He exemplifies a forensic functional rationality without the forensic denial that often goes with it. John's case is also particularly instructive in cases where a criminal functional rationality and substance abuse function in tandem.

It has been my experience as a criminologist that many substance abuse offenders commit violent acts less under the influence of a chemical substance, than the acting-out influence of the forensic functional rationality. Although there are some cases where heavy drug addicts commit violent acts with little or no capacity for self-control, there are many more wherein the offender has a great amount of self-control. They often act out their criminality according to the substance of a functional rationality hidden behind the appearance of an out of control addiction.

I would add in this addiction respect that the addictions that many offenders hide behind are not limited to chemical substance abuse. Addictions, be they chemical or non-chemical, such as deviant sexual predatory addictions, for example, are often driven by and deliberately fed by the offender. To the contrary, however, the offender usually presents himself as being compulsively driven by his inevitable addiction.

To present just one example related to the case before us in illustrating the forensic functional rationality and substance abuse addiction functioning in tandem, I recall a substance abuse offender with a life long history of attacking others while under the influence. In looking further into his case history, I noticed a strong functional pattern in his so-called compulsive, addiction-related violent behavior. Namely, this offender always attacked someone considerably weaker than himself...with a special focus on the women in his life. Although he committed all of his violent acts while under the influence, he never acted violently in any situation where there was the slightest chance that he might receive as much violence as he gave.

The reader is probably aware of the all too common situation of the Saturday night drunkard who returns home after drinking to beat the hell out of his wife or girlfriend. The reoccurring Saturday night abuse is often accompanied by the Sunday morning excuse that his drinking was the blame. John's case along with many others indicate that even serious and habitual acting out offenders with a substance abuse history have far more criminal intent, control and calculation behind their so-called and often miscalled "under the influence", addiction-related behavior than they'd like us to know. The major difference between them and John is that John has been unusually open and honest about it.

Addictive related criminal behavior can be rationalized in an addictive rationalization for doing what one cannot do in more rational situations. Beating up one's wife, when one's drinking or on drugs, is less blame-worthy to some than beating her up when one's sober or clean.

My analysis is by no means novel, just as Freud's Oedipus Complex was not new....in his adaptation of the Greek classic, Oedipus Rex. In an attempt not to be as analytically Freudian as the Freudians in making Freud's historical Freudian slip, I'll acknowledge the historical classical source of my analysis by referring to the original Roman source, In Vino Veritas, (In Wine Truth).

CASE 5: DOROTHY

PSYCHOLOGICAL EVALUATION

REASON FOR EVALUATION:
The evaluation was requested pursuant to a Court order to assess the Client's psychological capacity to resume caring for her daughter. The child, who will be six in January has been out of her care since she was three. The Division is seeking to terminate The Client's parental rights and she is contesting the action.

BASIS OF EVALUATION:
Rorschach Psycho diagnostic
Interview with the Client
Complaint for Guardianship by DAG
Reviewed but Not Relied Upon
DYFS Assessment: Parts I, II, B, Bs, printed 5/14/97
Case Summary for Transfer, 8/26/97
Placement Review Record, 12/2/97

BACKGROUND INFORMATION:
The following history was provided by Dorothy and has not been verified.
She was born in Newark but grew up in various localities in Middlesex County. She never knew her father. Her mother was drug and alcohol involved and could not maintain appropriate living quarters. From infancy till Dorothy

was about ten, the mother lived with a paramour who abused her and the three children: Dorothy, her sister who is one year older and her brother who is one year her junior. When Dorothy was about ten, her mother ended her relationship with that man and began another relationship with a man who helped her control her substance abuse and who has remained a positive influence in her life through the present time. Dorothy could recall only one time that her mother beat her and that was because she had been found with matches in school when she was about eight. When she appeared with bruises, DYFS investigated and began to monitor the family.

The children were placed in foster care for six months when Dorothy was about 11 after drug paraphernalia was found in the home. The mother, the mother's boyfriend and the brother moved to Florida to live with relatives when Dorothy was 15, after she had given birth to The Child. (She does not know why her mother moved but does not believe it was in reaction to The Child's birth because the mother was supportive at the time of delivery.) Dorothy writes to her mother and has monthly phone contact with her. Her brother did not finish high school but is employed and "doing OK." Her sister is "on the streets" in Middlesex County, drug involved and prostituting herself.

Dorothy was an acting-out, conduct problem in her early years in school but settled down and became an honor student from fifth grade until she quit in the ninth grade due to her pregnancy. She has not earned her high school equivalency diploma. She has no vocational training. Her employment history consists of four years of "under the table" work for family friends - the same people who now have The Child - who operate a kitchen remodeling business. She also worked for six months in a daycare center after she had lost the child and was refraining from drug use. She was not employed at the time of her incarceration.

Dorothy has never been married. The Child is her only child. She denied miscarriages and abortions. Dorothy began drinking beer and smoking marijuana when she was in middle childhood at the daily "parties" that her mother hosted. She also fraternized with older children who provided her with drugs and alcohol. When she was about 16 and after The Child was born, she was introduced to heroin by a male acquaintance and it became her drug of choice from that time on. In the last five years her longest period of abstinence has been just over a year, during the time she was in Florida with her mother and for six months after she returned to New Jersey. She returned to drug use at an undetermined time after visitation with The Child was suspended in May of 1996 and continued until she was incarcerated seven months ago. She has been through detoxification but has not completed a rehabilitation program.

Dorothy acknowledged a criminal history which includes charges of possession, distribution, prostitution and causing the death of another. She further acknowledged contempt citations in connection with some of these charges. She does not have a driver's license and denied motor vehicle violations.

Dorothy is currently serving two five-year sentences which run consecutively for the possession and induced death charges. She participates in substance abuse counseling. She is waiting for a class placement to work on her high school diploma. She expects to be transferred from maximum security to grounds status in the next two weeks. If the parole board agrees, she could be free by May of 1999.

OBSERVATIONS AND IMPRESSIONS:

Dorothy was evaluated in a classroom of the maximum-security unit of the Edna Mahan Correction Center. She is of average height (5'8") and weight (150 lbs.). She was dressed in state issue khaki pants, white T-shirt and athletic shoes. Her straight hair hung to the middle of her back. She work lipstick and eye makeup. She wore earrings and had what appeared to be braces on her teeth. There was nothing remarkable about her posture, stance or gait on brief observation. She spoke softly and displayed no unusual mannerisms. Her manner was unguarded and her eye contact was adequate.

Dorothy's intelligence appears to be within normal limits and possibly above average. She was alert and oriented in person, place and time. She understood the purpose of the evaluation and appeared capable of representing her own interests. Her memory for both recent and remote events was serviceable. Her associative processes were normally fluid and were not loose, tangential or bizarre. There was no evidence of psychotic processes or any disorder in the form of her thought.

Dorothy is in good health presently. She is not afflicted with any chronic medical conditions and takes no medication on a regular basis. She has no problem eating. She gets eight hours undisturbed sleep at night and feels rested in the morning. She denied psychological symptoms in the forms of obsessions, compulsions, phobias and psychotic experiences. She admitted to neither thoughts of suicide nor homicide.

Dorothy's mood was appropriately sober for the circumstances and sometimes became sad. Her affect was somewhat constricted but she did occasionally laugh and sometimes cried. Her self-control was adequate for the purposes of the evaluation. The nature and scope of the procedures as well as the limits of confidentiality were reviewed with Dorothy and she agreed to cooperate. The impression was that she was capable of producing valid and reliable findings.

PSYCHOMETRIC FINDINGS:

After being hand coded Dorothy's Rorschach responses were analyzed using the Rorschach Interpretation Assistance Program. Some of the phrasing in this report overlaps with the computer-generated statements. However, what has been highlighted and the emphasis given to it are my responsibility. Dorothy produced a record of sufficient length and complexity to be interpretively useful. The record contains no prominent clinical features and the analysis of her psychological organization and functioning shall proceed from the findings regarding her response style.

Dorothy's preferred approach to the problems of everyday living is strongly in the direction of detached analysis. In and of itself there is nothing abnormal or even unusual about this approach: approximately 40 percent of the population employs the same approach. However, Dorothy is somewhat extreme and rather inflexible in this regard. She is likely to use the approach even when a more intuitive, emotionally charged approach is in order. Moreover, style is not the same as capacity. Although she scans the environment for information as frequently as other adults, she processes what she perceives in a hasty, haphazard manner which does not give adequate attention to subtlety and nuance. When the situation is simple and straightforward, she can respond to it productively but she does not do well with complexity. In fact, her ability to read situations accurately is below that of the majority of the people to whom she was compared. Much of the distortion present is due to the idiosyncratic perspective with which she tends to view matters (a tendency frequently associated with drug use) but the majority of the distortion reflects clear violations of reality.

At first glance it would appear that not only is Dorothy in equilibrium but that she actually has an abundance of resources for dealing with the stresses of life. This finding is immediately suspect in view of her history and her own statements. Closer inspection shows that her resources are adequate but not abundant. What brings about the spurious impression of robustness is her below average stress level which she keeps low by a superficial analysis of life's demands and by the impulsive gratification of her appetites so that internal irritation does not develop. Although these tactics work to maintain homeostasis, they predispose her to make decisions which are not well thought out. Dorothy does not have an adequate command of her emotions. She prefers to keep emotions at a peripheral level and she constricts their expression to a degree that does not allow them to be available to fuel her goal-oriented behavior. Curiously, she appears drawn to emotional stimulation, perhaps as a way of experiencing vicariously what she will not allow herself to experience personally.

In spite of all that has happened to her and contrary to her statements, Dorothy's self-esteem is not markedly diminished. She is not very introspective ad her self-concept appears based more on imagination than actual experience. She appears to have the normally expected amount of interest in other people but again her conceptualizations of them are not very sophisticated. Two findings that are in apparent contrast: her expectation of positive interactions and her reluctance to become involved may be explained by her strong dependency. Dorothy prefers to maintain a passive stance in her relationships. She wants others to do her thinking and her acting for her as long as she can reap the benefits while avoiding the responsibility of her decisions. She also has a tendency to attempt to satisfy her needs in fantasy as opposed to actively pursuing her goals.

INTERVIEW WITH THE CLIENT:

The allegations of the Complaint were reviewed with Dorothy and she was given an opportunity to correct any misinformation and/or give her version of events. Dorothy denied that she had treated her then eight-month-old daughters in the manner alleged. She noted that The Child had no hair at the time and that the charge was unsubstantiated. Although she was using drugs at the time she did not use them in front of 16-month-old Child. She did pay the woman who cared for her daughter with drugs because that is what the woman asked for. She would not admit so to DYFS because she feared the consequences. It was not Dorothy but her sister who had her own son out late.

During a time when she believed herself pregnant, Dorothy nevertheless stored drugs in her vaginal canal. She did consider an abortion and ingested drugs during the period and found out that she was not pregnant only when she went for prenatal care.

The man identified as.... is actually Mr. O according to Dorothy and The Child had no reason to be fearful of him. She further denied that her daughter's personal hygiene was neglected. Dorothy represented that Ms. H used her as a convenient scapegoat for her family's problems during the time The Child and she lived in the H home. According to Dorothy Ms. H would not give The Child back to her and it was necessary for Dorothy to involve DYFS. It was Ms. H's own daughter who stole the money but Dorothy did sneak Mr. O into the family home. When asked about leaving The Child in the H daughter's care when the woman was allegedly drug involved, Dorothy replied, "Crystal took care of her all the time. When I left her with my daughter, she was not on drugs. I was out getting drugs".

After a brief stay in foster care mother and daughter went to live with the G Family. Dorothy promised to get help but did not comply. She joined her mother in Florida for a second time. She resolved the outstanding charges against her and remained drug free during that period. Around Christmas she returned to New Jersey because she wanted to help her sister who was heavily drug involved.

Dorothy denied that The Child was deprived and neglected while in her care. Yet moments later when confronted by the statements attributed to Mr. R (a man she does not know), she replied: "It's time though".

Dorothy was dismissed from a program for non attendance. She could not recall her whereabouts after that time until she met with DYFS at the G residence. She made a number of promises at that time which she subsequently failed to keep. She lasted two days in the Bergan Pines program before she was dismissed for smoking. When asked about why she left the G's, Dorothy replied, "when it really came down to it, I wanted to get high".

Dorothy essentially stipulated to the circumstances under which she lost The Child to foster care but explained that she had gone to the motel to "kick" the heroin in her system. She told DYFS that she had lost the telephone number of

The Child's caretaker so that she would not have to reveal the extent of her drug dependence. When asked about the apparent irresponsibility of a woman who would let a three-year-old wander into the street, Dorothy explained, "She had three kids of her own; I thought she would be responsible enough". Following The Child's removal, Dorothy detoxified and got some help for her addiction. In the light of sobriety she was embarrassed to have The Child see her deteriorated state. She doubts that The Child made the statements attributed to her because she never took her daughter to a bar although she allowed that she may have drunk in front of her.

Dorothy acknowledged The Child's severe acting out following placement; "she did it every time I left because she wanted to go with me". She enrolled in parenting classes and maintained her sobriety even after visitation was suspended. She had a visit four months later but started taking drugs again after visitation was suspended a second time. She may have been incarcerated at the time the matter was reviewed and therefore did not attend. Dorothy spent two weeks in jail on the possession/homicide charge before she was bailed out. She was subsequently indicted, arrested and incarcerated, released and re-incarcerated when the toxicology report on the victim was completed. When asked about her statements during that incarceration, Dorothy replied, "I was a mess".

Dorothy essentially stipulated to the six prongs of the Summary Allegation. She did say that she felt that she was cooperating with DYFS at the time visitation was suspended. At the time of this evaluation she has not seen The Child in more than two years. Although she does not blame the Court for its decision, she has a hard time understanding the reasoning behind it:

"All she wanted was to be with her mother. To take her away from me totally, I don't understand that. If a child's acting out because they want their mother, why take her away?"

In closing I asked Dorothy if she had anything additional to say on behalf of preserving her parental rights. She replied:

"All those allegations, though at that time, I was on drugs. I was on a very strong substance and I wasn't able to do anything right, not even care for my daughter. I did a lot of things that I wouldn't normally do unless I was on drugs. (But) I'm not on drugs anymore and I have no plans whatsoever about going back to drugs. I just want them to give me a chance to come out and show them that I will do whatever is necessary to keep my daughter."

DISCUSSION:

Dorothy has been evaluated in an effort to determine if she has the psychological capacity to be an adequate mother to her almost six-year-old daughter who has not been in her care for the last two and one-half years. Her history is the kind that is frequently revealed in termination of parental rights cases. She was emotionally neglected and physically abused. Her mother abandoned her when she was in her mid-teens. She has had no supportive relationships. She has little education and no occupational history. She has been drug involved all of her life having been introduced to drugs by the adults who frequented her mother's apartment. She has a criminal history connected with her drug dependence. She lost her daughter because of an act of negligence.

Dorothy's present psychological profile would not predict the irresponsible way she has lived her life (e.g., increasing her drug involvement after The Child's birth). To be sure there is much in her psychological functioning that needs improvement but the profile does not say in any conclusive way that she is mentally unfit to be a mother. A similar profile could be elicited from individuals whose parental rights are not in jeopardy. Although an unqualified statement to the effect that she does have the psychological capacity to be a parent is not justified by the psychological evidence, a statement to the contrary also cannot be made with the requisite degree of psychological certainty. The facts which are most damning to Dorothy come not from how she performed on a psychological test but how she has lived her life thus far with respect to her daughter, and much of that irresponsibility can be linked to drug use.

If the Court considers allowing Dorothy to retain her parental rights for the present on the assumption that she has the potential to improve her parenting ability through therapy, the decision needs to be informed by the following caveats. Dorothy grew up alone and unloved and never really had a childhood. Because of this she herself has been the most reliable person she has ever known. It will be very hard for her to trust someone enough to allow a therapeutic relationship to develop.

Dorothy is a "strong" person in the sense that she has found a way to maintain her psychological equilibrium and she will be reluctant to risk that equilibrium by investing herself in new ways of thinking and behaving. Dorothy has adequate self-esteem according to the testing. This suggests that she is comfortable with who she is and, therefore, not inclined toward self-scrutiny. Because of her good basic intelligence and essentially intact reality testing, she will be able to discern what is expected of her and be able to articulate the therapy goals. Whether Dorothy will be able to internalize the experience and profit from it in the long run remains to be seen.

FORENSIC ASSESSMENT:

Dorothy has overcome denial in squarely facing her addiction-related criminality. Her statement, "When it really came down to it, I wanted to get high," is an unusually honest self-appraisal of her criminality. The honesty that we see in her case and in the previous case of John is not usually seen by those who counsel criminals, male or female; and it is even more unusual among those with addiction related criminality.

Dorothy readily admits that she was not able to do anything right when she was on drugs, to include not being able to care for her daughter. She's faced that reality, in herself, and her intent, as stated, is not to go back to drugs whatsoever.

I'd like to comment that while it's been correctly observed that the road to hell is paved with good intentions, in forensics many of us tend to incorrectly assume that good intentions, per se, lead to hell.

Forensically, I would agree with the psychologist's emphasis on Dorothy's intact reality testing. The prognosis presents the right balance of a cautious affirmation of her prospects for success without being prematurely optimistic. One could describe the psychological analysis of her discernment and treatment goals articulation as the articulation of a core Reality Therapy approach...which would constitute the core of our forensic counseling approach as well.

The implication of this case, in particular, is that forensic assessment and psychological assessment can and should work together for the benefit of clients and offenders alike.

REFERENCES
(1) Ryan, Edward (1994). Cognitive Counseling in Criminal Justice, Journal of Instructional Psychology, 21, 4, 303-307.
(2) Ryan, Edward (1994). Therapeutic Justice and Child Abuse, Education, 114, 3, 328-336
(3) Ryan, Edward (1999). Forensic Counseling: To Be Or Not To Be? The Forensic Examiner, 8, 11 & 12, Nov-Dec 1999, p.34.

CHAPTER SEVEN

Chosinness and the Theology of Terror

In looking back to September 11th, we can look forward and back with a new word for a very new and very old Theology of Terror. Many religious and secular words have been used, but one new religious-secular word defines it best. That word is Chosinness, defined by me as a sinful choice wherein one God becomes one's God, only, to the detriment of others. That new word of Chosinness represents a metastasis of the old word of Chosenness, with the new meaning of a diseased distortion of the monotheistic concept of Chosenness into a "chosin" Theology of Crime contortion that sanctifies terrorism with theology.

Prior to September 11th, our monotheistic religions referred to an anti-God concept of evil; and since September 11th, there's been a new secular and religious adherence to an old intrinsic notion of evil . . . in particular, a pro-God proclaiming evil that evokes a God of Terror.

In any war, military intelligence is necessary; and in this Theology of Crime War, it involves the militant metaphysics of evil that our prior intelligence failed to protect us from. Those religious leaders who taught us that evil is a mystery we can't understand have failed us, just as those secular academics who taught us that evil is an unreal religious fantasy have failed us.

The one lesson we've all learned from September 11th is that "never again" should such failures prevail. Nevertheless, we still encounter failed religious and political homilies that fail our need for counter-intelligence and counter-terrorism. Immediately after September 11, we announced to one billion Muslims that we were not an enemy of Islam; and within a year, we broadcasted Jerry Falwell's religious defamation of the Prophet, Muhammad, as a "demonic inspired pedophile". This Jerry meandering Falwellian Chosinness turns our need for a "never again" counter defense into an "ever again" offensive religious encounter that generates more hatred and conflict.

I recall the prayerful invocation of "deliver us from evil," in calling for deliverance from the religious evil of falling into the well of a Falwellian Chosinness ... in creating the most religious enmity for us at the worst time in our history.

It's been said that war is too important to be left to the generals, and politics is too important to be left to the politicians; and it should also be said that religion is too important to be left to the likes of Jerry "Immoral Minority" Falwell.

We do need to pray for deliverance from evil, but in so doing, we also need to think about evil. The problem with countering evil is that our religious prohibitions against committing it, and our secular prohibitions against discussing it, have left us bereft of any analytic foundation with which we can encounter it so as to counter it. The unfortunate consequence is that in attempting, but failing, to prohibit evil thoughts, we've succeeded in prohibiting attempts to really think about evil ... in prohibiting any thoughts about evil in prohibiting evil thoughts.

September 11 made us face our failures in facing up to the necessity of better counter-intelligence for the purpose of better counter-terrorism. After September 11, no one could escape the realization that evil is all too real, and that our Theology of Crime War is all too religious.

I use the word "evil" in its most literal sense from the inverted spelling of "live." This terrorist inversion of life, in the literal taking of thousands of lives, can best be understood as the criminal metaphysic of Chosinness. Evil is an appropriate secular and religious word, for evil doers have done what no others have done before in bringing the ultimate evil terror of a Theology of Crime Chosinness to our shores. That criminal belief system of Chosinness must be encountered in order for counter-terrorism to succeed at the same level from which the Theology of Crime terror proceeds.

The best defense is an offense aimed at the complex points of origin of our enemy ... Chosinness. Offensive religious descriptions of the Falwellian ilk are not only invidiously simplistic, but they are insidiously dangerous in making us more simple targets for the more simple minded. Simplistic axis of evil political responses escapes the complex reality and meaning of evil in its varying commissions of wrong and omissions of right. A crusading simplicity will inevitably fail us, but it may well succeed in further endangering and isolating us.

Evil is a real religious notion and the real axis of evil revokes around religious inspired and politically implemented notions of Chosinness ... in choosing one God as one's God for one's group, only, at the expense of others!

Enemies naturally regard each other as evil, but even if one's enemy is truly evil that natural good versus evil dichotomy obscures the not so natural nature of evil. Human nature is not evil, as Calvin taught, but one's nature becomes evil the more Chosin one is taught to become. There's often a reciprocal Chosinness of Terror wherein a metaphysical oneness is chosen by one group for themselves to the detriment of another, who then respond with their own Chosinness of Terror.

Simplistic religious assumptions about more of God and simplistic secular assumptions about less of God have proclaimed more wrong answers in the name of both pro-God and anti-God perspectives than right questions. The right questions are those that ask all of us for new perspectives with which we can name our religious God or secular Good, so as to break the "chosin" cycle of terror . . . for once and for all.

In contrast to the pre-September 11th criminal profile of a terrorist with nothing to lose, the Theology of Crime Terrorists had much to lose in the here and now . . . but even more to gain in the hereafter. At least one of them, in addition to being quite mature and well situated, pursued advanced studies at Germany's premier institute of engineering. In that respect, he reminded me of Nazi mass murderers, such as Josef Goebbels, Ph.D. and the Angel of Death, Josef Mengele, M.D., Ph.D. I include their academic and scientific credentials to illustrate that mass murder, high intelligence and elite education can coexist quite easily.

The Chosinness of the Theology of Crime terrorism is new for most Americans; but it's not new for Israelis, in being victimized by this "chosin" criminal belief rationality emanating from some in the Arab Muslim world, as well as some in their own Jewish world, to include the Chosin People who assassinated the political leader of the Chosen People, Prime Minister Yitzhah Rabin. It is not new in Northern Ireland, in not only so-called militant Catholic and Protestant bombers, but also in religious parades wherein one group celebrates victory by denigrating another with the refrain that "God is with us but not with you". It's not new for Armenian Christians, over a million of whom were massacred by Muslim Turks; just as it's not new for Bosnian Muslims in being ethnically cleansed by some of the Chosin among the so-called Christian Serbs, who described themselves as Chosen in defending Christianity against Islam. Just as the highly educated Arab terrorist reminds me of highly educated Nazi terrorists, and just as the assassins of Yitzhak Rabin evoke highly educated Judeo-Nazi terrorism, the Chosin terrorists who ethnically cleansed Bosnian Muslims had their own well educated political leader in Radovan Karadzic, M.D.

Our greatest enemy is not a remnant of godless Communism, or Nazism, but a terrorist who believes that God is on his or her side. This enemy attacks with a Chosin metaphysic that is a metastasis of universal Chosenness, defined as a universal spiritual choice wherein God is chosen by and for all men and women without any invidious distinction. Chosinness turns the choice of one God into a choice of one God as one's God, only . . . in turning one God for all into one's God against all others. That is the root cause of the Chosin metaphysic that drives the Theology of Crime; and whenever and wherever it transcends itself to others, it descends upon them with its terror. It can descend upon anyone from within a plane, a militant group, an oppressive state, a denigrating creed, a racist nationalism or an international cause . . . in the name of God or a Godlike substitute.

Is there something we can do to counter this etiology of terror now and in the future? Yes, but it requires something other than one group telling itself how terrible another group can be. It requires every group telling itself how terrible any Chosinness can be, to include its own; and it requires defenders of the faith in Chosenness, for all, fighting those defenders of a faith in Chosinness for themselves to the detriment of others. Those defenders must be spiritual firefighters who rush to the twin towers of religiocentricity and ethnocentricity to put out any cinders of Chosinness before they spread. In so doing, Muslims need to preach to Muslims, as do Jews to Jews and Christians to Christians rather than one group preaching at another. Secular humanists need to be reminded that while terrible people have always brought terror in the name of God, there is no God of Terror. Our politicians have to be cautioned that when they entangle America in group conflicts, most particularly religious conflicts, their political understanding must go beyond standing for what's right for one side to standing for what's right for all sides.

We cannot fight terror from without, without fighting it from within. We cannot be terrorized by fear, nor terrorize in fear. The right question as to how to counter the terror of self-serving Chosinness requires the right answer within us and with others. That answer requires more spiritual warriors to help fight against the God-awful metastasis of a terrorist's God, without allowing a God of Terror to win within ourselves. The spiritual war strategy must be that of convincing the next generation that God is with us, but God is not with us if we believe God is with us only. Anyone or any group who falsely teach that they own God to the detriment of others must be taught that God has disowned them.

CHAPTER EIGHT

Forensic Counseling: A New Approach to School Crime

Forensic Counseling, as defined by Dr. E. Scott Ryan, can be understood as counseling of offenders, both juvenile and adult, in a manner that does not repeat past treatment and education failures. Dr. Ryan describes the medical model treatment mistake of relying upon mental health professionals to treat crime and delinquency as if there were an illness they could cure. These therapeutic rehabilitative approaches have failed for the simple reason that an offender in trouble is not necessarily a troubled offender. Accordingly, a criminological or delinquent pathology, as observed in a criminal or delinquent ego, cannot be equated with a psychological or psychiatric pathology. In addition to the failures of specific medical model approaches, the inappropriateness of general moral education approaches is also addressed. Rather than purporting to teach secular or religious morality in a pluralistic society, with the concordant pitfalls of moral dissensus and conflict, forensic counseling concentrates on the specific criminal rationality dynamics associated with criminal rationalities and rationalizations in a direct but not denigrating manner, so as to counter them before they become worse and to reverse them with continued forensic counseling and treatment approaches.

After being invited to present my workshop on Forensic Counseling at The New Jersey Education Association's annual conference in Atlantic City, the largest education meeting in the world, I was informed, I realized the remarkable largely untapped educational potential for responding to crime and delinquency. Despite the frustration of having not only to teach, but to discipline, the educators in attendance among the approximately 55,000 NJRA members were not only not frustrated, but quite enthusiastic. Many of them asked me what they could do next, and that is why I am responding with my suggestions. The fact that the Governor was there was an immense plus.

First, Forensic Counseling can be understood as counseling for offenders, both juveniles and adults, in a manner that does not repeat our society's failure to respond effectively in the past. (5) Despite our best intentions, we have failed to deal with our problems of crime and delinquency, and casting the failure in terms of liberal versus conservative approaches is quite mistaken. The mistakes that have been made can be grouped into one of two approaches: the first one of being too specific in the wrong way, and the second of being too general in the wrong way.

The Medical Model

In reference to the first mistake, we have relied upon mental health professionals to treat crime and delinquency as if there were an illness that they could cure. We know in criminology that crime is not an illness and that it cannot be cured by what we refer to as "the medical model". We have attempted to employ medical model pathologies and failed for the simple reason that an offender in trouble is not necessarily a troubled offender. There are some troubled people in all walks of life, but a criminal or delinquent pathology is not a psychiatric or psychological pathology. Dr. Thomas Szasz, MD. in his book, Psychiatric Justice (10), followed by Dr. William Glasser, MD, in his book, Reality Therapy (2), and myself in my article, "Therapeutic Justice" (9), and in my books on Forensic Counseling (4)(7), all come to the same conclusion and can demonstrate why the medical model has failed to work. Although Szasz and Glasser are doctors of psychiatry and I am a doctor of criminology, we have come to the same conclusion regarding the failure of rehabilitative therapeutic counseling in treating crime and delinquency. A school psychologist or psychiatrist has a place in treating mental pathology whether it is associated with delinquent or non-delinquent behavior. That is a very specific task, but it is not the same task of dealing with crime and delinquency. The application of specific therapeutic rehabilitative treatment based upon the medical model accounts for the fact that treatment has not worked. Nevertheless, the fact that the wrong treatment has not worked should not lead to the erroneous conclusion, as it has among many, that there is no way to treat crime and delinquency. (6) We can treat delinquency with forensic counseling, and educators can be trained to do this fairly quickly at a fraction of the cost of traditional treatment programs (3)...that have failed for decades. I shall say more about that and how the educational system can respond after explaining the second mistake.

As is often the case in reacting to insoluble problems, in swinging from one extreme to another, some treatment programs have gone from specific mental illness pathologies to simplistic moral pathologies. Instead of the first mistake of employing pseudo-medical diagnosis with specific psychiatric or psychological terminology, a second mistake of employing a general moralizing approach is taken. In some correctional programs, inmates carry around their moral reflection notebooks to record their supposed moral progress.

THE MORAL MODEL

Morality is important but an educator is not a moral guru and should not pretend to be one. Further, the problem to be addressed in dealing with crime and delinquency is not a general moral one, but, rather, a very specific one of criminal rationality and rationalization. One does not need to be a mental health professional as in the first failed approach, nor does one need to be a moral educator as in the unrealistic and simplistic second approach.

In fact, introducing a moral education approach is fraught with not only failure but danger. If one employs secular morality, it is neither convincing nor strong enough; and if one employs religious morality it can be divisive and discriminatory. In neither case does it deal with the problem of crime and delinquency in the manner that is effective and one that reflects our pluralistic society.

I am not arguing against the moral component in many faith based crime fighting community programs. In fact, in my first book on forensic counseling (4), I pointed to successful faith based community programs among Baptists and Muslims, in addition to effective Catholic programs. I recommended cooperation among these various programs in working together to combat not only crime and delinquency but hate based extremism on the part of some secular ideologues and some religious zealots.

One should remember, however, that the Sept. 11 terrorists represent both a new and old Theology of Terror criminal belief system that has manifested itself in many different religious belief systems; and I have discussed that criminality in my book, The Theology of Crime. (8)

Once educators assume the role of moral educators they open themselves up to moral analysis that can lead to absolutist positions based upon sacrosanct positions. It should be noted that the most dangerous criminals are and always have been those who believed that God was on their side. Moral education should be left to religious and faith based communities and not introduced into public education when the education task at hand concerns crime and delinquency.

When Irish Catholics first arrived in America, they reacted negatively to the Protestantism in the public schools by establishing their own Catholic schools. In pursuing the moralist education approach to dealing with crime and delinquency, we are opening the door to competing and often conflicting moralities. The simple idea that morality is good and therefore all good people will be of one moral accord is simplistic to say the least. Since those who disagree with the politically correct morality are not likely to be able to establish their own school system in response, the conflicts will simmer within and could easily become an independent group conflict precipitator. We already have some clerics preaching hate, in the name of morality, as chaplains in our correctional institutions. (1) Morally, can you prove that they are wrong? Can you morally prove it to those who agree with them and not you? Think about that conflict scenario which is already here and try to keep it out of our schools, please! It is a sham that has nothing to do with effective criminological counseling in our schools, and it has dangerous implications in reference to engendering ideological and moral belief system based conflict and criminality.

Forensic Counseling

Fortunately, we have a new alternative approach of Forensic Counseling that is effective and does not repeat the therapeutic mistakes of the first misstep or the simplistic moral assumptions of the second misstep. Educators can be quickly introduced to the principles and procedures, which are based upon criminological facts rather than model medical or moral assumptions. Forensic Counseling teams consisting of three or more trained individuals can be created with no more than one seminar and one workshop preparation. I would recommend that these teams be established in every school and in every institution that deals with crime and/or delinquency. Techniques can be adapted to the respective needs of varying schools and institutions. The result will be not only improved school safety, but better school services in general, in enabling more forensic counseling to combat delinquency at its incipient stages before it gets out of control.

The word penitentiary stems from the Quaker concept of imprisonment being one of doing penance for crime in meditating upon the evil on one's criminal ways. The Quakers have always tried to do right even when they were not right in imposing solitary confinement as a means of prisoners doing penance. Nevertheless, more often than not they have been right, as they are now in stating that we are robbing the school house to pay for the jail house. Forensic counseling allows us to stop robbing ourselves of a new approach in enabling us to both save money and reduce delinquency and crime as soon as they surface in our schools and society.

Educators, in particular, can be trained as forensic counselors in encountering the criminal rationalities and rationalizations associated with crime and delinquency in such a manner as to counter them before they get worse. This forensic counseling approach is far more effective than any other and it is far less expensive to implement. It is a criminological no-brainer for any jurisdiction that has considerable brains at both the educational and political levels.

REFERENCES
(1) Barrett, Paul M., "How a Chaplain Spread Extremism to an Inmate Flock," Wall Street Journal, Feb. 5, 2003, pgs. A1 & A13.
(2) Glasser, William, Reality Therapy, Harper and Row, New York, 1975.
(3) Kolstad, R. and Ryan, E.S., "Forensic Intervention Counseling Training for School Personnel", Scientia Paedagogica Experimentalis, XXXVI, 1, Universitiet Gent: Belgium, 1999, pgs. 145-149.
(4) Ryan, E. Scott, A Forensic Counseling Approach, Anchor, Lancaster, VA 2001.
(5) Ryan, Edward, "Cognitive Counseling in Criminal Justice", Journal of Instructional Psychology, 21, 4, Dec 1994, pgs. 303-307.
(6) Ryan, E. Scott, "Forensic Counseling", The Forensic Examiner, 8, 11 & 12, Nov-Dec 1999, p. 34.
(7) Ryan, E. Scott, Juvenile Forensic Counseling, Anchor, Lancaster, VA 2002.
(8) Ryan, E. Scott, The Theology of Crime and The Paradox of Freedom, Anchor, Lancaster, VA second edition, 2003.
(9) Ryan, Edward, "Therapeutic Justice and Child Abuse", Education, 114, 3, Spring 1994, pgs. 328-336.
(10) Szasz, Thomas, Psychiatric Justice, MacMillan, New York, 1965.

www.ingramcontent.com/pod-product-compliance
Lightning Source LLC
Chambersburg PA
CBHW080551170426
43195CB00016B/2748